HUGS & HOPES
for a century

by Sara Sanderson

*For Ann & David,
another century wouldn't be long enough, to tell about all the wonderful times we've shared, the somber times carried, dreams hoped for!
Love always,
Sara Sanderson*

HUGS & HOPES
for a century
©1998 by SARA SANDERSON

ALL RIGHTS RESERVED

Library of Congress
Catalog Card Number: 98-90796

ISBN: 1-57579-129-3

Printed in the United States of America

PINE HILL PRESS, INC.
Freeman, S. Dak. 57029

for Tyler, who believes

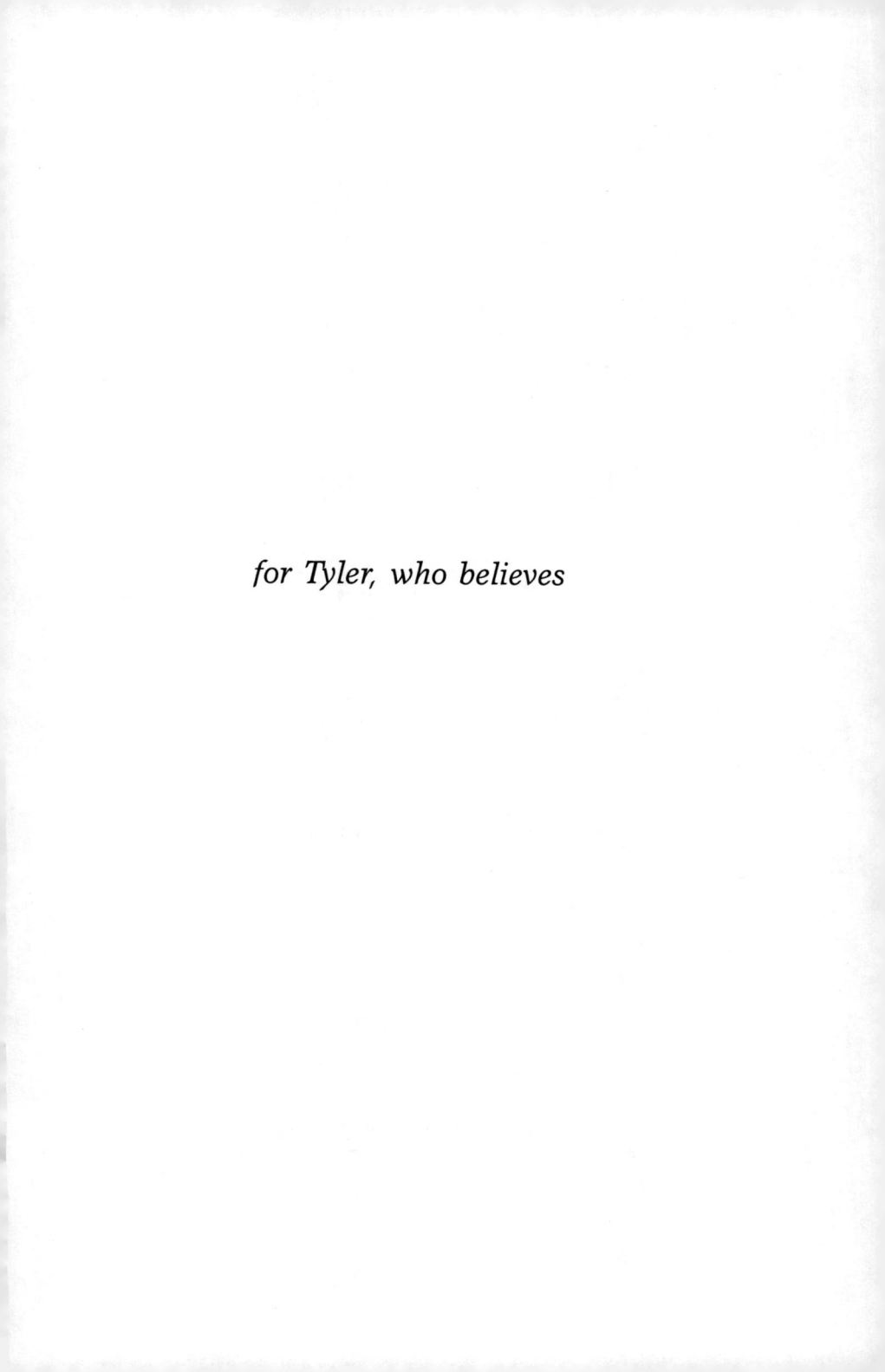

ACKNOWLEDGMENTS

I hug all those whose voice or effort contributed to this offering; their names appear alphabetically. Some interviews appear as a single entry, some are scattered in several sections, some are combined in spirit with others. Thank you, all.

John Aleshire
Judy Barrett
Laura Beito
the cab driver, Bobby
Beth Bonham
Marty Boyd
Patte Braker
Phil Bremen
Camilla Hull Brown
Tom and Sandy Brown
Barbara Burton
Rob Compton
Shirley Cosson
Chuck Cottle
Jane Daniels
Virginia Day
Heather Dilley, of Pine Hill Press Inc.
Barb and Bill Dodge
Doris Douglas
the election workers, November 1995, Ward 19:
    Patti, Don, Nancy, and Shirley
Tom and Mary Ellis
Ivan Enchevich
Leonard Flath
Mary Ellen Fox
Carole Gall
Winford Galmon
Ruth Gluckman
Ralph Gray
Beth VanVorst Greene
Rev. Richard E. Hamilton
the quilters at Handcrafts Unlimited:
    Vivian, Joyce, Marjorie, Pat, & Vida
the bunch at Hardee's:
    Alma, Chet, both Johns, and Wanda

Donna Harrill
Michael Heavener
Bob Helberg
Karen Rush Hill
Andy Jacobs, Jr.
the buffet cashier, Jason
Bishop Reuben P. Job
Dottie Kiehle
Amy Knoebel
Bill Kurker
Bill Landon
Elizabeth Langston
Elaine Lentz
Richard E. Lindseth, M.D.
Harry and Mary Lee Mamlin
The Moonbow Lady
Sue Morris
Betty New
The Parasol Lady
Ken Pench
Merrill Person
Tomio Petrosky
Jeanette Piske
Jill Richardson
Kenny and Greta Sanderson
Hal and Carlie Saunders
the students at Schreiner College:
    Courtney, Debbie, Arisha, Mandy, Marisa,
    Tammy, Thomas, JC, Heather
Dick and Sue Shankle
Richard Silwedel
Mabel Sims
Bob and Jeanne Slobod
David M. Smith, M.D.
Jay Southwick
Jackie Speicher
Paula Underwood Spencer
Chris Stillo
Billy Ray Stubblefield
Helen L. Thomas
Charles and Nancy Walkup
Tyler, Adam, and Mandi Wessel
Jim West
Mark White
Vic White
Harold Winkler
Skip Wood

Down deep we all hug something. The great forest hugs its silence. The sea and the air hug the spilled cries of sea-birds.
from *Klee Wyck*, by Emily Carr
©1941,1986 Irwin Publishing
Toronto, Canada

Nothing that is worth doing can be achieved in our lifetime, therefore we must be saved by hope.
attributed to Reinhold Niebuhr
(1892-1971)

TABLE OF CONTENTS

1. Connecting Memories 1
2. Back When I Was In School 6
3. The Larger Family Gathered 10
4. Home, Hearth, and Hideaway 17
5. The Warmth of Quilts 24
6. Down On The Farm 29
7. Hair Today, Gone Tomorrow 34
8. Dear Santa 40
9. Don't Tell Our Secrets 44
10. Letters, We've Got Letters 49
11. Meet Me For Coffee 54
12. At The Fair 61
13. These Newfangled Inventions 67
14. Our Heroes 76
15. We're Passionate About Life 81
16. Honest Hard Work 89
17. Seeking Wisdom 93
18. Volunteer To Get It Done 101
19. With Liberty and Justice For All ... 107
20. Remember To Vote 118
21. Healing Ways 127
22. The Music Around Us 133
23. Our Planet 143
24. Our Faith 147
25. Our Tomorrow 156

PREFACE

Turn-of-the-century, a new millennium, call it what you will, by any name it comes as opportunity.

Catch the daily news; you may sense our situation — and therefore our future — bleak. But perhaps these are not the worst of times; perhaps it is a chance to reflect. I began, over two years ago, starting to think about what we've done right; what we can celebrate about the century we knew. And then, I wondered, what would we hope, for those who will walk after us?

The idea for this book grew: I wanted to create an album of voices, a record of hope instead of gloom, to leave for posterity. So I began calling friends, highlighting maps, traveling, and talking to anyone who'd smile back at me. Two things happened: one, I met wonderful people, and two, I found out we — as collective people — are full of hope.

At first, I imagined there might be regional differences, perhaps noticeable demarcations between our varied pasts and our images of the future. The marvelous results proved me wrong. What became apparent was a true patchwork quilt of love, stitched of many colorful opinions — each one unique, but forming amazing patterns.

The threads increased, from busboy to bishop, mall walker to welder, physicist to house painter. There's a college student, and the ninety-three-year-old mother of my former college roomate. There's a World War II bomber pilot, a homeless woman, a labor union organizer, and a massage therapist. Neighbors, relatives, and strangers spoke up; as individuals they may have encountered roadblocks, sorrow, and pain. Yet these people responded with such hope, it made my heart sing.

The quilt grew, from patches added in Charlotte, North Carolina; Knoxville, Tennessee; Bensalem, Pennsylvania; Cincinnati, Ohio; Potomac, Maryland; Pageland, South Carolina; Venice, Florida; Indianapolis, Indiana; Nashville, Indiana; Nashville, Tennessee; Austin, Texas; Georgetown, Texas; Kerrville, Texas; Redmond, Washington; Seattle, Washington; Vancouver, British Columbia; and San Anselmo, California.

I met Laura on an airplane over Minnesota, Bobby in a cab in Tennessee, and Harold on a Greyhound bus rolling through North Carolina. I chatted with Richard in a deli in Texas; I shared wine in Ivan's Canadian home. I rode the evening ferry out of Seattle, the bus out of Austin, and I walked the bridge from Kentucky into Cincinnati. Everywhere I went, people were gracious, willing to share. "You just *have* to talk to..." was the usual offer.

Perhaps as you read this, you are curled up in your favorite chair. Perhaps you are standing by a display in that wonderful new bookstore, thinking Aunt Peg would laugh over the part you just read. That is exactly the point: dip in, read at random, share it with someone.

And now, I invite you to participate. I've left some empty spaces in the book, tucked in for you. Here's your chance, this is your place to write in memories and ideas. I wish I could include a box of crayons with every book; please find some, and make your part fun.

I cherish every person who contributed, every insight they shared. Savoring, saving, and sharing; that's what I think it's about.

Connecting Memories

☆♥☆

Many of our treasured memories from this century come from ordinary events. Who does not remember Grandma's button box, which you could ask for when sick in bed, to sort and pile on the coverlet? We keep an old black-and-white snapshot of our first Chevy, or our 4-H project blue ribbon. We remember doing homework on an oilcloth-covered kitchen table, during air-raid drills. The rest of the house dark, the kitchen windows covered by a black shade; Mom did dishes, Dad read the paper, and you answered the questions at the end of Chapter Twelve, snug in the haven of one room and three hearts.

The memories we hug rise back into focus, coaxed by a summer rain shower, an aroma of banana bread, or a golden-oldies tune on late-night radio.

Connecting memories and weaving them into patterns of vision celebrates every one of us; it becomes our gift to ourselves.

☆♥☆

☆♥☆

It was one of those drenching rains, darkening the short ride from an economy motel to the Greyhound Bus station. Intrigued by my questions, Bobby, a cab driver in Knoxville, Tennessee, pulled his vehicle over onto the gravel shoulder of the road, turned off the meter, threw his arm across the seat-back, and reminisced: "Wadda you wanna know?"

> "Home is the place where, when you have to go there, They have to take you in."
> —Robert Frost: "The Death of the Hired Man"

Head back, he laughed. "Oh yea. I'm almost half a century. Already lost all but two of my nine brothers, sisters. Both ma' parents. But I learned one thing — cherish your loved ones while they're alive — 'n don't get too caught up in alla this stuff."

Bobby gazed somewhere beyond the rain, talked about family dinners, and plank tables — "You know, planks spread 'cross sawhorses, in the yard, to feed the field hands, at noon." He grinned, listing "fried chicken, oh yeah — green beans, hoecakes, and sweet potato pie." What he treasures most, though, is that "we all sat and *listened* to each other!"

> Bill, a hair-stylist in Indianapolis, treasures memories of train rides: "going with my sister, to visit our aunt; the window-framed farms, the speed, the noise."

He paused, and thought a moment. "We all gonna have our trials 'n tribulations, but," he continued, "sun's gonna shine tomorrow!" Bobby laughed. "Now what book is this I'm gonna look for to buy? That I'm gonna be in?" Bobby laughed, some more.

☆♥☆

This space is reserved for you. What was on your family's picnic table? Which uncle or aunt told those funny stories?

It Came Far

It's raining;
fat bulging drops smash
like pudding dropped from a spoon.
Washing through the years,
rain streaks the cottage window
of my childhood.
I see my mother in that creaky chair
pulled up to view the waves that are
crashing out the storm.
Jubilant, her soul watered
by the event,
she blossoms.
Sand gnats swirl around a lamp,
plummet to patterned oilcloth
on the heavy table. I move
my paper dolls,
begin their lives again.
Daddy, long limbs folded, hunches
before the grate,
pokes alive the fire,
looks up to announce we're in for
only a three-day blow.
I hug the damp smell
of wet sand
this time-warp moment brings.
Now I'm in a land-locked apartment,

I shut the patio door,
rain continues.
It came far.

☆❤☆

> *Mary Lee,*
> *a tutor and*
> *mentor, in*
> *Charlotte, NC,*
> *treasures family*
> *— "that lap of*
> *encircling values,*
> *your umbrella*
> *of support."*

BACK WHEN I WAS IN SCHOOL

☆♥☆

Janet, a librarian, residing in Indianapolis, Indiana, reminisces about school:

"With Mom working evenings, I was home from college to take John to the Jefferson Elementary School Fall Carnival. My brother didn't complain about going with his sister, even though most kids came with two parents which was the norm in those days.

"When I saw dads in the gym shooting basketballs at the free-throw booth, I felt compelled to compensate for my brother's fatherlessness. I knew how to shoot a basket. I could make one and win the prize of a fat pretzel stick as well as any dad.

"Despite John's wary expression, I paid my quarter, stepped behind the table, and took aim. The ball left my hand on target, just a little short.

> When Frank W. Cyr conducted a transportation study in 1937, he found that children rode to school in everything from trucks to horse-drawn wagons. Cyr's safety rules established the school bus standard bright yellow color, still seen today.

It hit the front rim and shot back toward me whonking the edge of the table. The jolt collapsed one pair of table legs and catapulted the plastic jar of pretzels.

"Two dozen salted jumbo pretzel sticks flew over my head and hovered like alien missiles. They crashed to the hardwood seconds before the student body sprawled, grabbing for pieces. John was the only kid not on the floor giggling in salt and crumbs. John was gone.

"I ran from the gym. I searched classrooms. I looked in the janitor's closet. I paid a fourth-grader to check the boy's bathroom. On my way to notify teachers, John found me.

"He smiled and handed me a cake. He had taken refuge in a cakewalk upstairs and stayed long enough to win an angelfood and forgive me.

"I never won my brother a pretzel. But, I gave him a most-embarrassing-moment story in which he did nothing stupid."

☆♥☆

⭐❤️⭐

Many pensive gazes and spreading smiles crop up when the subject turns to *"back when I was in school."* Remember the large jar of white paste, doled out with a sticky ruler onto squares of paper at each desk? Remember scratching out lines of OOOO's with a straight pen, so proud you could now use ink? For the younger children, those round inkwell holes in the right-hand corner of the desk remained empty. But, oh, rapture, in the third grade, you graduated to an ink bottle to fill the hole!

> *September, 1905:* The Campbell Soup Kids first appeared, in an ad in the Ladies' Home Journal.

Ah, and that feeling, as August burned to summer's close and the drugstore filled with school supplies; soon...soon we would find our new classroom and learn which teacher we'd have for the year. "Who'd YOU get?" we screamed to each other, on the bus.

September never rolled around without a new box of crayons; remember the wax smell, the perfect points? This year you'd *really* keep them nice. Brand-new meant also new clothes — kindergarten plaids, in crayon and fall-leaf colors, sixth-grade saddle shoes that you polished with that chalky white stuff. The high school guys were "in" if they

> *Those NECCO Confectionary Company favorites, the little hearts that say "Be Mine" or "Say Yes" or "Sweet Talk" were invented in 1901.*

wore charcoal gray slacks and, of course, white bucks. Cool, Man.

Sunday evening, we got-ready-for-school. We made sure our lunch money was laid out, our homework done, and we figured out what to wear Monday. Let's see, if you saved the green sweater for Assembly, on Friday, then...

"Now children, take out a fresh sheet of paper." Get ready. Begin.

☆❤☆

The Larger Family Gathered

☆♥☆

Church socials, block parties, family reunions; our century celebrated well. In a fellowship hall, at a Harvest Festival occasioned to kick off their church centennial, we listened to
> Chris,
> a handbell ringer,
> a gift of giggles,
> in Redmond, Washington.

Chris remembers living in a big house, selling it, learning — as many of us have this century, "all the trappings aren't important. Our priorities have changed!"

Blond curls bouncing, giggles as bubbly as the casseroles we directed to two lines of serving tables, Chris cherishes family. The church hall in the basement, the gathering of a community...Chris has a very large family now. And she wants us to know this "good solid relationship with God and each other."

Baked beans arrive; someone brought deviled eggs. Aproned men are lined up behind the serving window counter, carving turkeys, making gravy. Do we have enough rolls? Where should we put the cranberry sauce? Chris, and the other ladies, choose places along the tables for their family plates and silverware. The larger family gathered, to celebrate another Harvest.

☆♥☆

> "Increase, O God, the Spirit of neighborliness among us that in peril we may uphold one another, in calamity serve one another, in suffering tend one another, and in homelessness and loneliness and in exile befriend one another. Grant us brave and enduring hearts that we may strengthen one another, till the disciplines and testing of these days be ended."
> —*prayer used in Air Raid Shelters in England during World War II*

☆♥☆

Elaine,
a church custodian,
in Charlotte, North Carolina,
was sure the room was ready for the gathering after a memorial service. Another church, all the way across our vast United States, another row of serving tables ready. Elaine has a moment to sit down, while the service continues upstairs.

What does she treasure from this century?... church. Singing in the choir, youth fellowship, even going to Europe on singing tours. She remembers "my family *always* came; they all did. We did everything...covered dish dinners...kids playing ball." Church, home, neighborhood; it flowed together.

> *"Life only demands from the strength you possess."*
> —*Dag Hammerskjold*

Elaine leans back on her folding chair; trim blue jeans, crisp print shirt, tailored vest appropriate for the days event, mind alert to "Is the coffeemaker coming on too soon? Is there a mike for the speakers?"

Up for a chore, back, to continue. Up for a task and back, to rest and watch for the crowd to file in. "Family did more, in my time. Schools. My family *always* came to meet the teachers. 'Cause I love my parents so much, it meant *so* much to me for the *teacher* to meet *them*."

She thinks a moment, brings out more pitchers of water, settles down again, to her memories. "I was bused in the ninth grade. Some said I coulda boycotted, but I didn't. It was okay — it hadda happen."

Elaine hugs her childhood, worries about all the anger we see today. "They cover up the love they have inside theirselves." Elaine knows what would help: "I been hurt too. So deeply, I thought I'll never let anyone in again." But still, "I said to Stella it's almost like we're angels or sumthin' — we're here for a *reason*." Elaine knows she is growing stronger and stronger, firmly avows "I can still do something!"

One, two, then a straggling line of mourning family and friends enter the room, winding down the staircase from the sanctuary. Elaine rises, smiles, and gets back to work. And another chance to "do something."

> "No one can live on grief. Yesterday is yesterday, tomorrow is tomorrow."
>
> "You left out today."
>
> "Today is already yesterday."
>
> —1952 movie: *Affair in Trinidad*, starring Rita Hayworth

☆♥☆

☆♥☆

Dick,
of Auburn, Indiana,
is the father of my new
daughter-in-law,
so now family, himself.

Dick remembers a heritage of family gatherings, often at funerals, or weddings:

"When a death occurred, all the family was notified and expected to return for the viewing and funeral. Much food was prepared and all of the cousins got reacquainted with uncles, aunts, etc. Hymn sings took place along with a 'celebration' because death was assumed to be passing on to new and different things — hopefully, heaven.

"While the body of the deceased was usually kept in the home, the small towns and villages of rural Pennsylvania supported the family with gifts of food, visits, and then the processional to the church for the final words.

"Quickly the mood often changed after the minister left the home at the conclusion of the funeral dinner. Sometimes someone produced some 'spirits.'

> Nancy, a clerk at the polls, election '95 in Indianapolis, knows: "We are so blessed to have the support and love of family and friends. My husband is a blessing in my life. I pray my children and grandchildren have friends, family and spouses to support them in life."

As a child, I remember these same family events would often occur at weddings as well, and all were expected to attend.

"The dignity of people," is what Dick treasures today. "Each person's life is unique in a special way." And, at the end, family gathered to celebrate at the funeral.

☆♥☆

How many places are you part of family? What are your rituals and traditions?

Grandma's Garden

All she knew was kids 'n Grandpa,
screen-door summers,
clothespin bucket,
and a little 'un at her feet.
Now he's gone.
They say "Move on".
Oh sure. Where *to*?
But most of all, with *who*?
Beside the house the cornfield rustles;
dry leaves no longer green
remind her all the years
they'd seen
planted, waited, then the harvest.
cycle now to be no more.
Tired, she weeps
"What's left in store?"
Grandma, hold on to Spring;
Apple blossoms,
returning robins,
misty rain to coax the lawn.
There's a grandchild's baby
to be born this winter, an infant
to bring to life's garden
another Spring.
One who needs your stories told
on porch swing days,
to give growing years
strong roots
and ways.

> *Karen, a volunteer at a handcraft shop in Georgetown, Texas, remembers "going to Grandma's." She adds, "She'd **never** raise her voice, there'd be a line and we **knew** not to cross it!"*

HOME, HEARTH AND HIDEAWAY

☆♥☆

Vic, doorman at a luxury condominium in Austin, Texas, shares Dick's and Elaine's love of family. "My wife sets a table that reaches from here, across the street." Now, thirty-one of Vic's family live within walking distance of each other in Austin; they have all retired here. Years ago, Vic was the first, moving his wife and son from New Jersey, opening up two ice cream parlors, selling them, buying a motor home, and traveling "the whole country."

Vic jumps up from his desk in the lobby, keys the elevator call system, opens the front door for another resident. A glance at the security monitor, then he continues:

"My son — he's now a senior sergeant in the police department — has bought a twenty-six-foot cabin cruiser, 'n we make a pot of coffee, 'n go out, 'n just *sit*."

Vic has two daughters, who will be the last to arrive in Austin. "They're on the East Coast. Soon as their husbands retire, they'll come!"

Vic sees our future becoming more fragmented. He foresees fewer family members living near one another. "The main thing is, we should get along." He knows we must disregard color, pull together "like a big puzzle. If there's a part missing, you can't see the picture."

Now, if we could all move to Austin, we already have relatives. Vic's arms, heart, and table are waiting.

☆❤☆

☆♥☆

Families, big houses, and togetherness; sometimes, however, we craved a secret hideaway. Tree houses, forts stamped out in deep snow, trails to "jungle camps" in the side lot, this was the stuff of dreams.

Such a secret hiding place, for me, was in the closet, in that little house on Boardman. Inside, the built-in boxed shelf on the right was much like a window seat, without the window. I always wished it were a treasure chest, or anything at all, but it didn't really open, so I could only guess at what might be inside.

I did love, though, to climb up on top of it, my heavy oxford shoes thumping hollow tones deep within. That was the place to play "What if...?" What if someone who lived here before us had killed someone, and stuffed him inside, and *that's* why the lid was nailed down? What if someone had hidden a lot of money in there? Every once in a while, I would feel along the edges, trying to find a latch or secret opening; of course, there never was one.

> *"The future belongs to those who believe in the beauty of their dreams."*
> —*Eleanor Roosevelt*

My mother sometimes walked into the room, quite surprised when my answer to "Where *are* you?" came muffled from behind clothes in the closet: *"Here!"*

"What are you *doing* in there?" I didn't really want to answer "Sitting here thinking about being a special little girl General whom all the soldiers adore." So I'd reply "Nothing." And silently wish, "Oh, please, please, go away."

☆♥☆

Tom,
"a seventy-six-year-old man,
loving each new day,"
lives in Seattle, Washington.

Tom recalls side-lot baseball games, backyard basketball games, and balmy summer evenings standing under the street light on the corner with buddies. No organized, uniformed, sponsored and ranked teams; pick-up games with your friends filled the summer.

"Mother was always home when we came in," Tom reminisced. "Dinner was the time the family of five discussed what each had done during the day. Life was rich."

You have to walk fast, today, to keep up with Tom, as his long legs stride ahead of the early morning mall-walkers. Tom talks, as we walk, about his days as a pilot during World War II. "I flew planes to Alaska," he explains; "and I flew 'The Hump' into China." Tom does not live in the past, however; his passion is the future, and the values he hopes he can represent to his grandchildren.

"That old neighborhood is something I hope we get back to," he muses. "that place where you couldn't get away with something that your parents did not hear about."

Everyone knew you, everyone cared. Tom does.

That old neighborhood: Who lived next door? Did your ball ever go through someone's window? Where was your secret hideaway?

> "Would it have been worthwhile,
> After the sunsets and the dooryards and the
> sprinkled streets,
> After the novels,
> after the teacups,
> after the skirts
> that trail along
> the floor...."
>
> —T.S. Eliot:
> "The Love Song
> of J. Alfred
> Prufrock"

☆♥☆

Basements, ah — the storehouse of memories. Over there, near the tubs lining the northwest corner, we used to have the wringer-washer. I would watch, fascinated, as my mother fed the steaming clothes in one side, and a flat ribbon of tangled fabric came out its jaws.

Behind the stairs was an alcove, raw wood shelves holding an assortment of vases and bowls. "Go down and get me the green pansy bowl" sent one of us girls to search its wares, usually calling back: "I can't *find* it!" "Last time I knew, it was right there — by the Christmas Madonna. Look again!" We did, and it was.

Over in the northeast corner was the old fruit cellar, behind creaking doors. We never had rows of home-canned peaches or beans; we stacked *National Geographic*s on its shelves. Oh, those fascinating photos of tribal people *with no clothes on*! And those wonderful maps; we dreamed of voyages to those dots with strange names.

Outside the fruit cellar, we stacked a winter's cord of firewood, Dad's store of small jars containing nails, his tools, and various paint cans. Lots of things remained there for years, "just in case we needed it."

Beyond the clotheslines gridding the main room, we kept barrels of cut-glass bowls, hand-painted fruit plates, and bouillon cups; inheritance of an only daughter, of another only daughter, to pass down later to two girls.

> "I've been things, and seen **places!**"
> —Mae West
> in I'm No Angel
> 1933

There was the black trunk my mother took to a private girls' school, then college. Now, it held a faded silk dress from Civil War days, one I squeezed into for a Junior High skit. Its rustle of aged cream and brown striped silk made me feel perhaps I was the ghost. The trunk also held the Civil War coat of a distant relative; we decided to save the buttons. Mother had a bracelet made for herself, and screwback earrings for us girls. We had to ask Dad what the sword and funny red hat were for; he evaded true answers, keeping Shriner secrets from little girls' pryings.

> "To the memory, nothing is ever really lost."
> —Eudora Welty

We peeked, poked, dreamed, and wondered. This was real stuff. Touch, and connect.

☆♥☆

The Warmth of Quilts

☆♥☆

Five ladies were seated around a quilting frame, heads down, fingers flying over the fabric. They looked up, as I entered the shop. I asked if I could watch, and then perhaps ask them a question. "Sure! Pull up a chair." I did. Vivian, Joyce, Marjorie, Pat, and Vida, were working on a quilt sampler. They said, "Each one of us's working on a different pattern."

> A trademark we know well, Elsie the Cow debuted as a cartoon character in medical journal ads in 1937. Bordon Co. brought her "in the flesh" to the 1939 World's Fair in New York.

They worked in a handcraft shop on Courthouse Square, in Georgetown, Texas.

I inquired about the designs. "Oh, let's see,"Vida answered: "This one's 'Nosegay,' that's 'Honeybee.'" Smiling proudly, she said, "and I'm workin' on 'Little Dutch Girl.'" One of them turned the whole frame over: "Remember? We did 'Jacob's Ladder,' here, and 'Flower Garden' and 'Sunburst'?"

Vivian kept on sewing, thought about what she hopes for the next century, and paused. "Teach the younger generation what you know, and they'll do it. Like quilting! My two daughters do, but the grandkids don't. We never taught them." She smiled at her daughter, seated across from her, and poked her needle back into the taut fabric, squeaking its way into another tiny stitch.

☆❤☆

> *In the 1920s, in Fremont, Michigan, Mrs. Dan Gerber asked her husband if he could adapt the machinery at his tomato puree plant to make strained peas for their baby Sally. Dan, and his father Frank, could — and did. Five varieties of strained fruit and vegetables were the first baby foods offered.*

☆♥☆

In 1993, I wrote in my journal:
"This weekend I was struck by another tie to these things that really make life rich. I was caretaking the antiques in Boot's flea-market booth, grumping a little over how often I had to refold the quilts.

> *1912 —*
> *Oreo cookies appear on the market.*

It seems everyone — I mean everyone — has to open out or ruffle them all. Then it dawned on me — the quilts actually *pull in* the fingers, seek the caress; the tiny stitches of their original making call for other hands. Love pats adding to the creation of more warmth — no wonder we love to snuggle in a quilt. We need the hug."

> *1933 —*
> *The debut of Skippy peanut butter.*

☆♥☆

> *1937 —*
> *Kraft macaroni and cheese first offered.*

> *1940 —*
> *M&M candies introduced for the first time.*

☆ ♥ ☆

That 1993 journal was special: padded calico cover fancier than my usual spiral-bound notebook. One blustery January day, I wrote —

"Busy, happy times. Lunch last Saturday with David; he had brought me some wonderful beads, from New York City. What a fabulous time he had there!

As we were walking along Market Street, we encountered a bag-lady, huddled turtle-like deep in her coats. Her quilts and things were neatly folded, in a grocery cart, nearby. We said hello, and walked on.

About a block later, I admitted I wasn't feeling right, that I hadn't offered her food. And there she was — right in front of Steak 'n Shake. With definite emphasis where it belonged, David glared at me — "It's *not* too late."

Yes, but...busy schedule...my bus... "It's *not* too late," he insisted. We walked back. "Excuse me..."

Up came the turtle head.

"I didn't do what I *meant* to, a moment ago; would you like a sandwich?"

Smiles and giggles; no, she'd had some coffee.

> "A culture will be remembered for its warriors, philosophers, artists, heroes and heroines of all callings, but in order to survive it needs survivors... still... carrying on."
>
> —Bill Reid
> Haida sculptor,
> British Columbia,
> Canada

She showed me the empty cup.

"More coffee, then? Anything?" Yes, she nodded: "Would you hold my hand?"

Wow. Out of the depths of her clothes came a warm, smooth, nut-brown hand. I knelt beside her bench, took her hand. We looked into each other's eyes. "Bless you, bless you," she insisted.

Later that night I remembered: she had *quilts!* No wonder, I was pulled back, to her touch."

☆❤☆

Your thoughts and memories of quilts:

Down On The Farm

☆♥☆

We spread across our land this century, moving beyond the Mississippi to points west. The migration continued, in a new way: we started leaving the farm for the city.
           Charles,
           a music teacher
           in Charlotte, North Carolina
warmly remembers our farms. We talked about growing up able to run barefoot in soft, warm, loam and watching Daddy plow the field. We talked about the reverence with which a good farmer sifts a handful of soil through worn fingers, testing its readiness for the seed. The smells, the textures, the warmth of good earth, are part of Charles's fondest memories.

We were seated on the floor of a friend's living room; what former farm boy needs a chair? Charles looked startled, stopped his coffee mug in midair, and exclaimed, "My son calls it *dirt*!"

Seems young son had been asked to weed the front walkway, but quit. "Why didn't you finish," he was asked. "Because I can't stand this *dirt* all over me!" he replied.

Charles wants us to remember the wonder of holding good *earth* in your hands, and to walk barefoot through warm fields once again.

☆♥☆

> *September 1926 —*
> *The first set of the*
> *18" x 40" Burma-Shave*
> *signs appeared on U.S.*
> *Hwy. 65, near Lakeville,*
> *Minnesota.*
>
> *"Men with whiskers*
> *'Neath their noses*
> *Oughta have to*
> *Kiss like Eskimoses"*
> —*Burma-Shave*

☆♥☆

Bill,
a computer systems manager,
in Redmond, Washington,
recalls his grandfather, foreman for a large ranch, the man with "that farmer's hardness, you know, the hard shell, with the soft inside."

Bill and his wife Jill roam the Pacific Northwest these days, on their Honda Gold Wing; he fishes Alaskan wilderness, with a buddy. But his reverence for the beauty of our earth began in fields of lettuce, wheat, or soybeans, following a wise old man.

The moral values this grandfather passed on are what Bill hopes the next century will treasure. Listen, and walk those rows of memory with him; perhaps, we'll hear the old man whisper yet.

☆♥☆

⭐❤⭐

Bob,
a retired petroleum engineer,
lives in Kerrville, Texas.

Bob actually bought a farm.

During his years as a professor at Penn State University, he wanted his children to benefit from the freedom experienced, and lessons learned, in tending that which once was a necessary way of life.

"They did learn," he thinks back; "they learned to mow hay only when it's dry, they learned how to bale, load a wagon, and stack it at the barn." It was a good time, Bob reflects.

Doing something well, learning new skills; of course, that included getting your cow out of the neighbor's garden. But there were built-in rewards at the end of day; horses for riding, a spring and pond "off to the side," a huge maple tree for climbing.

Ah, yes, and "one of the best stands, anywhere, of watercress." Who could want more?

⭐❤⭐

Ah, the farm. Was it Grandpa's? Dad's? Is it yours now? Write all about it here — the long nights, lemonade on a hot summer afternoon, mending a harness. Tell the story of our land.

HAIR TODAY, GONE TOMORROW

☆❤☆

Oh, the lengths to which we go: frying our locks on electric perm-machine rods in the Forties, looking like our dogs, in the Fifties (did *you* have a poodle-cut?). Two of our contributors have hair-raising tales to share. No, not hair-raising as in horror-movie fright; they offer stories about their hair, as they were being raised, as youngsters.

    Jane,
     who, today, has gorgeous hair,
     and lives in Indianapolis,
remembers that her mother taught her "the value, joy and beauty" of good hair care.

  Cistern water, those precious raindrops, was collected in a barrel; you washed your hair ONLY with cistern water. A pitcherful or two, dipped from the barrel kept just outside the back door, a basin, and you were in business.

  Of course, you washed with the bar of Ivory Soap, and you added vinegar to the rinse. Hair was an asset, to be well-treated, and preserved. Jane remembers the little nightcaps her mother made, that you wore to bed, every night. "Protect your hair" and "Keep it in place" were her stated reasons.

Of course, a little girl also felt cozy in its hug.

☆♥☆

Which special haircut do you remember?

⭐❤️⭐

Jeanne, elegant, today, with short silver hair, lives in Kerrville, Texas, and was about seven, when she took her first stand of independence. She writes:

"I was the baby of the family. There were always older siblings to shepherd and boss me around — to make decisions; to go off to mysterious places I was not yet allowed to go; to lock me out of the bathroom every now and then. I didn't even go to school. Each morning after lunch boxes were filled and the others left, I took my schoolbooks up to Grandma's room for my 'lessons.' I was enfolded in an exceedingly loving, caring — and busy — household; but I was the littlest one there."

"I had golden curls in those early days which mother would gently brush around her finger. Who knows why I decided the curls had to go. It certainly wasn't vanity.

I don't remember what wiles I may have used or just what it finally took to convince the family that it was time to cut my hair. But the day did come. A large chunk of the family trooped with me over to the home of our best family friends where amateur cutter, Helen, about my eldest sister's age, agreed to do the job. It was a simple cut. Just a few whack, whack, whacks. No styling — nothing fancy, such as bangs. Just stubble. Then she brushed it back in place and refixed the barrette.

"Weeping, my mother gathered up the golden ringlets, wrapped them in tissue paper, and put them away. I was ever so sorry to make her cry, but I was not sorry to lose the curls. Suddenly, I was no longer the 'baby.' From then and hence forth, I was me."

☆❤☆

★♥★

Awareness of connections is one of Jeanne's gifts. Fifty years later, she recognized this old tie to independence, as her locks were shorn once more.

"Well along up in my fifties," Jeanne recalls, "I was now consorting with a super group of people, largely women, who gathered for board and committee meetings in Washington, D.C. Our organization was out on the cutting edge of working with women in developing countries and provided a stimulating atmosphere for my education and growth.

"At one of our board meetings, our president, Katy, arrived to preside with an astonishing new haircut. Her pale gold waves had been sheared close to her head. How did she ever have the nerve to take such a drastic step!

"Katy had been invited, she told us, to be a member of one of the very first select groups to be allowed into China following the Nixon dramatic opening visit there. She had no idea what the facilities might be like in that part of the inscrutable Orient. She did not want to waste any precious time having to deal with hair and curlers. So, practical Katy cut her hair as short as possible.

"At first I was aghast; then I was greatly admiring of her courage. Later, I decided her face was more interesting unadorned by a distracting head of hair. A seed was definitely planted.

"Wouldn't it be wonderful to be able to shampoo, blow dry and be off and about my business or my pleasure.

"On the other hand, was my face capable of surviving naked of coiffed waves and curls. And besides, Bob would hate it. To cut or not to cut was the question. Finally we found ourselves in Austin for a stay. The vast expanse of my native Texas encouraged me to be daring. I said to myself: 'It's now or never, I don't care whether anyone else likes it or not. It's my face, my hair. I'll do it and if it's too bad there'll be time for it to grow back before going back east.'

"And so, I did it. It was even more liberating than when I was seven. It wasn't completely easy, of course — nothing ever is. At first, a blow dryer in my hand turned hair into a horror. After some experimenting, I learned how to tame it. I don't think I'll need another major hairstyle again."

☆♥☆

Dear Santa

☆♥☆

Ralph,
a writer and historian,
in Indianapolis, Indiana,
cherishes Christmas, snuggled in the hug of a close family. Ralph notes:

"I realize now what a privilege I had to live with my parents and siblings in my grandmother's house — didn't everyone live with best-loved relatives?"

Ralph continues, about this maternal grandmother: wise, literate, compassionate, "and quite literally the most important person in the tiny southern Indiana village of Otwell. As the editor and chief writer of the community newspaper, a weekly that consumed her life but not to the point of being unavailable to her family (after all, the editorial office, conference room, and mailing room of the paper was also the front room of our house), she kept her finger on the pulse of the community.

> *The game of Monopoly, based on Atlantic City, New Jersey, went on sale December 1, 1935.*

"Each year, with the approach of winter and the cheery fires carefully laid in the small fireplace that warmed our multi-purpose front room, the entire family eagerly anticipated the Advent season, the gathering of relatives from faraway Jasper and Petersburg at our house on Christmas Day, and of course Santa's arrival earlier that same day.

"But how could I inform Santa of what I needed for Christmas? Grandmother's answer was simply write him a letter or just a list and give it to the elves, his helpers, who frequented our fireplace, living just above and behind the curved structure at the base of the chimney. She often saw them there, and I did too, once or twice, but they were wispy and shy and difficult to see clearly.

"One year, as I was sending my carefully printed list to Santa, by letting it float above the flames and start up the chimney where the elves would get it, I let go too soon and my letter burned. Grandmother was quick to assure me that she would see to it that Santa would receive her copy of my list, and indeed she did, and Santa duly delivered many of the desired items."

At age 13, Godtfred Christiansen joined the family toy business called Lego, which meant "play well" in Danish. In 1949, he began making the plastic bricks still popular today.

☆❤☆

☆♥☆

Beth,

writer, prayer-friend, and

someone who knows the

wisdom of play,

lives in Indianapolis, Indiana.

Beth remembers what we girls dreamed of, a Christmas doll. That ecstatic moment, creeping downstairs Christmas morning, when you spied her. Just for you, this replica of all your dreams. Beth recalls two of the best —

"Jane had brown eyes and an abundance of red hair curled and puffed a la Jane Withers. When I first met her, she wore a straw hat, a multi-colored candy-striped dress with a sash of the same material. She had a complete set of underwear, lacy and silky, white silky socks, and Mary Janes! I had patent leather Mary Janes for weddings, funerals, and church (bought large so they would 'last'), but the undies were a revelation to a girl who was wearing — and would continue to wear for a few years yet — cotton pantywaists designed to hold up my sturdy brown cotton school stockings and white cotton dress-ups. She was joined in the next year, my seventh, I believe, by Betsy, the name being my early childhood nickname: Betsy Bobbin.

"Betsy, looking like a girl-child as all dolls did, wore a blue dress and white pinafore. Her blond hair was dressed in two glorious braids, tied with teensy blue ribbons. As the year before when I tried to curl my wispy blond hair like Jane's, I tried to spit-curl, gel, and lacquer my blond strings into a braid with poufy bangs in front.

"Jane and Betsy live in my heart and I fondly recall other forays and adventures with them in the rites of my passage into teenhood: grooming, talking about boys, primping in front of the bathroom mirror doing terrible things to my face and eye lashes with orange Tangee lipstick (forbidden) and my mother's eyelash curler. One day I made them my willing, smiling accomplices in my first bout with fingernail polish. I practiced on their lips and nails. Forgiving as they are, they continue to smile through bright red little lips, showing pearly white teeth, and giggle with me, their little red-nailed hands covering their mouths."

Jane and Betsy now reside in Beth's cedar chest, and might come out for short visits, if you're lucky enough to be invited for tea.

☆♥☆

DON'T TELL OUR SECRETS

☆❤☆

It shocks some, today, that private e-mail messages remain in cyberspace, and can be picked up, later, by police detectives tracking a suspect. Whatever happened to "now promise, you won't tell a *soul*"?
    Mary,
       an energetic elder,
       whose hobby is *people*,
       now lives in Redmond, Washington.

Mary led the pace, as we rounded a corner of stores on the second level of the mall. It was "before hours," and the mall-walkers owned the space. Mary's elegant pink jogging suit was easy to spot, when we arrived. Silver curls, radiant smile, easy stride: yep — there's Mary! Catching up, we walked, and talked.

"You remember," she mentioned, "that I told you the story of our little-granddaughter who made the remark that she didn't have anyone to talk to, so we sent her a clown rag doll, and she told her secrets to it...and it *didn't ever tell them.*"

Mary continued, "Well, I think now-days we need to 'hug' those friends who never tell a secret." She added: "Very few people seem to be able to do that...you know — news is news!"

With a glance and a big grin, she moved on.

☆♥☆

Add your secrets here — we won't tell!

☆❤☆

Mary Lee,
lover of all children,
tutor and role model for many,
lives in Charlotte, North Carolina.

Mary Lee's best friend, as a child? — a tree. Yes, a tree. Growing up in west Asheville, she had her choice of several; there were the tulip poplar, the apple and the pear, and lots of climbing.

There was the "sarvus" tree (serviceberry); you *could* climb it, but didn't; it was better for sitting under, or playing house. And the oak: "too tall to climb, but my father threw a rope over one limb, to make a swing." Often, Mary Lee would meet her best friend at "the pink tree" (a redbud). She remembers both, well.

Mary Lee hopes every child today, and tomorrow, have "some spot of *sanctuary*," as she did nestled in the cocoon of a lofty perch in that apple tree. Best friends are wonderful, but a tree keeps secrets, too.

☆❤☆

☆♥☆

Talk, talk, talk; it's all around us. Buy this, park only in the red zone, take out a number-two pencil; will they ever shut up? And yet, our century will be remembered for another kind of talking — real conversation, face to face, side by side, during an evening stroll, or real-in-person on the phone. Now we opt for a "menu" of computerized voice-mail options. Already, some software experts meet once a week for "talk salons" at a local restaurant; seems we still crave contact.

Brad, twenty-nine,
an insurance adjustor
for the city of Charlotte,
North Carolina,
called about the accident I had witnessed; he wanted some information. But then, so did I, so it was a fair exchange.

What does he want us to cherish, from this century? He said, "Talking with each other." And we did.

Separated by cities, demographics, most everything, one poet and one insurance adjustor found out we were both raised in western New York State, specifically, Buffalo for one, Syracuse, the other. We both loved the Adirondacks, further east.

Brad explained: "Everyone at work has little cubicles." He misses "presence," he says; the chance to be together, sharing.

☆♥☆

      Liz,
      a listener,
      a licensed private-practice
      psychologist,
      in Kerrville, Texas,
leaned against the wing-backed armchair, sighed, and closed her eyes. The smile spread, giving away images forming behind those resting lids:

"Small town stories," Liz began. "I remember a mother, a father, Ms. Wolf, Aunt Mary...always time to talk to a child."

She sat up, opened her eyes, and continued, "They painted pictures, for me, of other places, of dreams of the past." There was more; we settled back into family arms, cradling memories of voices from the past.

☆♥☆

LETTERS, WE'VE GOT LETTERS

★♥★

Jill,
a recent MBA degree holder,
and spirit-seeking person,
lives in Redmond, Washington.

Jill feels loved and cared for, every time she re-reads the letters her mother and father wrote, over two-thousand miles away, and spanning many years.

"They wanted to stay close to me and share with me all the activities they were doing. They thought talking on the phone was *too* expensive. I got *detailed* accounts of what was made for dinners and where their journeys took them. I still have these letters and look through them occasionally. I have a calming feeling that floods over me when I read them. My parents had such love and concern for me, and it showed in their faithful letter writing."

Virginia, energetic community activist, in Redmond, WA, treasures having her own letters, mailed home from college. Her mother saved them, and gave them back.

Jill hopes that tomorrow's children aren't adrift in the world; she prays that they get letters, and that "they feel loved and cared for as I was — even from across the U.S."

A letter from Jill arrived this week; she included a newspaper clipping on Vancouver, a place we both love. She shared her recent doings, asked about mine. I'd better stop here, so I can write Jill, before the mailman comes.

☆♥☆

People I should write to, today:

★ ♥ ☆

Rob,
a labor-union organizer,
sat in the gallery above
the Indiana House
of Representatives
While we waited for the session to resume, we played with words. What if a character in a novel, that I haven't written yet but want to, had sacks full of words that she loved, and dispensed as necessary? He joined my search. Long lists formed, on a yellow legal-pad, divided into columns headed "soft," "exciting," "mystery," or "verbs to give," "adjectives," and even "memory."

Under "soft," I had already put down "lap . . . sugar cookie . . . kitten . . . breeze." Rob took the pad, thought a while, adding: "harp . . . silk . . . baby."

We moved on. Under "exciting," my list included "trumpet . . . thunder . . . blade." That one was easy for Rob: "travel . . . pulsing . . . rocket."

The legislators were still milling around, down below, and we continued. Rob penciled in "plaid," and "amber," under adjectives.

Under "verbs to give," where I had inserted

> *"The greatest discovery of my generation is that human beings can alter their lives by altering their attitudes of mind."*
> —William James

"promise . . . renew . . . cherish," the young labor union advocate added: "strive" and "dramatize."

Oops! The gavel fell. Session called to order. Much less fun than our own word search, ponderous debate took over.

☆♥☆

My list of yummy words to savor:

☆♥☆

Jason,
a college student, working
as a cashier at the
state park inn
just outside Nashville,
Indiana,
hopes there will be room in the future for a poet.

On a misty, chilling day, as deep autumn settled into the Brown County hills, a refilled mug of coffee and a window-side table in the Inn were the perfect spot for a writer. Jason came over, to talk.

"Last night," he said, "I went deer-hunting." As he had, for the past five evenings. But mostly, "sitting up there in my tree," he confided, "I watched the sunset." Ah, yes, that magnificent crimson glory, of the night before; I had been enraptured of it, too.

"What I really think is, I should write about it," he proposes. Stopping a minute...reflecting, Jason asks, "Do you think there'll be room in the future for a poet?"

I hope so, Jason; I hope so.

☆♥☆

MEET ME FOR COFFEE

☆♥☆

In small towns, they meet at Marge's Diner, swap yarns, and sip coffee all morning. You know: the heavy white coffee mugs, the corner table reserved for "The Boys," and the easy laughter.

"Heck, you ain't goin' *nowhere*, Charlie. Set *down!*"

Okay, so in the cities across our land, many of the breakfast buddies now meet at one of the fast-food burger places that sell breakfast; the coffee comes in foam cups, but if you want to, why, bring your own mug.

☆♥☆

> *1900 —*
> *The first roast, ground coffee packed in vacuum tins was developed by Hills Brothers, in San Francisco.*

Just Us Guys

Cafe table,
tan and white oilcloth,
four mugs before four men.
Work-weathered Elder smiles;
comfort folded in his
red-and-black-checked
hunter's shirt, his khaki jacket
with the American flag
on the sleeve.
Beside him, in denim jacket,
jeans, and High Tops,
hair spiked and tailed,
another of the regulars works valiantly
to get his chin
higher than the table.
A very solemn five-year-old;
one of the guys.
He sighs;
this guy stuff is hard to understand.
He tries,
glad when it's time to rise,
and leave.

✩ ♥ ✩

John,
Alma,
Don,
Chet,
Wanda,
and a second John,
meet every morning at Hardee's,
in Indianapolis, Indiana.

"Hey, whatcha writing today?" one calls over to my table. So I mention the book, slide over to an empty swivel chair near Chet, and open a fresh page in my journal. "Go ahead. Ask us." The fun begins.

John leads off with "radio, and your imagination." Soon, they all chime in, one voice leading to another: "Amos 'n Andy, Fibber McGee & Molly, Red Skelton! Orson Welles, Lux Theater, Inner Sanctum. Oh yeah! — Edgar Bergen and what was...what was his dummy's name?"

"Charlie McCarthy, that's it!" The voices went silent, then picked up again. At the mention of "Tom Mix!" someone else remembered: "The Lone Ranger!" And there was one vote for "WLS, out of Chicago, with the best country music this side of

*1900 —
The hamburger was invented when Louis Lassen ground 7¢/lb. beef, broiled it, and served it between two slices of toast, at his little three-seat restaurant, "Louis Lunch" in New Haven, Connecticut.*

heaven."

Radio programs winding down, Alma brought the crowd to a new topic: "games! Hide and Go Seek, Run-Through, Hop Scotch..." Wanda got in on the deal: "Spin-The-Bottle, and Tiddly Winks, and paper dolls — I designed my own. Kick the Can, and tin-can stilts," and, she closed, "Monopoly!"

John, in the corner, had been listening; not joining in, but listening. Everyone knows John gets the little table by the window, and everyone knows he does the newspaper crossword puzzle first, before he chats. John already had a pen, so he reached for my paper, and wrote:

"Victory celebrations, baseball, track, basketball, get-togethers for good talk and joking, love, romance...as a teenager." Wanda looked at his list. Seeing the word "Victory," she jumped in, adding: "and World War II victory gardens, to 'help the effort.'" Everyone agreed; we remembered those.

Chet started us off again: "Ooga-ooga horns, on your automobiles!" John added: "Sling shots! — we made 'em with a broom stick, a nail, and an innertube strip." The conversation continued as a duet: "Putting coins on the railroad track, and waiting for the train to smash 'em. Railroad steam engines; we'd lay beside the tracks and wait for them. Or we'd lay at night, the windows open. *Loved* the wail of the night train coming through."

"Model T, and the Model A, Fords."

"Yea, and our Lionel trains: Pennsylvania, B&O."

"Streetcars ran downa middle of the street. And trolleys. We'd run behind 'em and jump and pull the 'lectric cord."

"We'd ride to school on the horse-drawn hack."

Transportation over with, it didn't take a second to round a new curve: *"music!"* someone offered. "Al Jolson, Benny Goodman, Glenn Miller, Ernest Tubbs, Hank Williams, Little Jimmy Dickens, Jimmy Rogers, Lulu Belle and Scotty."

"Oh yeah, Margaret Whiting. Jack Jones. The Andrews Sisters, Dick Haymes, Don Ameche, Dick Powell."

Music floated to "what we wore" then; I knew about corduroy knickers, bib overalls, and smocked dresses; they had to explain to me how to double-roll socks, and what "leggers" were — those spats that came up like boot-tops.

They wore Chesterfield coats, Stetson hats, and a white silk scarf with fringe; Mary Jane shoes, bloomers, and a muff to match your coat and leggings.

We heard, in detail, about the "Navy Junior" pea coat, the "one with little ribbons that spelled dot-dash-dot, the secret Morse Code."

We settled down into private musings, separate memories drifting around the table:

"The old pickle barrel."

"The flour barrel."

"The big old porcelain coffee pot."

Just the mention of porcelain, and a chorus chirped in: "Porcelain kitchen table! Pie Safes! Our early icebox! And those black- or red-rimmed kettles!"

So we got to homemade butter. The washboard, and boiling clothes. "Feeding" the clothes wringer. Memory ran deeper, as the group leaned back into their own seats. Alma smiled shyly, began talking about "Grandpa, who came on the weekend. We'd all sit around the fire; he'd tell scary stories."

Meaning "for mica," the laminated plastic used for kitchen counters, known as "Formica," was developed in 1913 by Herbert Faber and Dan O'Connor. Faber came up with the product's name.

Someone else picked up the thread of sitting around, talking, and added:

"Wakes! The men would sit up drinking, all night. At home. We were comfortable with death."

Silence fell again. Someone moved on: "Making lye soap, on Friday. Scrubbing floors with corn husks, then pure white sand." A laugh: "Then, we got *linoleum!*"

"Coal stove, fed it corncobs soaked in kerosene. Warming oven, side bin of hot water. Tin bathtub, behind the stove." More laughter: "You wanted to be *first!*"

We lived "up the lane," and "down on the farm," and we wrote to Aunt Marge, sending her news for a three-cent stamp. "Your handshake was your *bond*," John nodded, for emphasis.

No one had room for any more coffee; one by one, we said "Well, I gotta go," and "See 'ya tomorrow!" The last one to leave turned at the door, to call back to me — "Fairs! Don't forget to put down 'Fairs'!"

I promised I would remember.

☆❤☆

AT THE FAIR

☆♥☆

The county fair belongs to everyone. Whether you won a blue ribbon once, for your persimmon jam, or are a city-slicker visitor, we love the carnival atmosphere, the flannel shirts and "Howdy!" grins. At the 1994 Marion County Fair, outside Indianapolis, Indiana, this is what I found:
— concrete floors, clean sawdust, and a girl sitting on her pig
— The Lions Club booth, offering roasted ears of corn, a dollar each
— square dancers, skirts a twirl of gingham over lace panties, caller requesting:
"side through side,
face to face,
back to back,
slow basketball turn,
now slow vine three..."
— families, sleeping bags and coolers, an electric fan, and their livestock, all bedded down for the night
— the "Bible Quiz Book" booth, next to the

"John Layton for Sheriff" table

— a demonstrator, teaching anyone willing to watch for an hour, how to flat-reed a chair seat

— one little girl, sequined dress and gobs of rouge and eye make-up, tap dancing to "Jesus Loves Me"

— beyond the Hot-rod Tractor Pull, a sunset over the semis on a highway

— farmers and good ol' boys, on bleachers for the tractor pull — "Hey! They gotta Stihl chain-saw motor on it, with a *turbo*charger! Hell, it's just a brain rush for them boys, that's all."

Balloons, fried "elephant ears," and pigs squealing; oh please, please take me to the Fair!

☆♥☆

What do you love to do, at the Fair?

☆♥☆

Move on, to the State Fair. Your quilt or cow won the County; now the stakes are higher. The buildings are permanent, the carnival rides and booths a whole small city of lights.

Look around: savor the flashing neon, listen to the riders' gleeful screams. Step carefully, over snaking coils of electric cable, puddles of ice cream, litter of denuded corn cobs.

Beyond the Midway, stop at a "Lemon Shake-up" stand, devour the aroma of charcoaled pork chops, the sizzle of Italian sausage and green peppers. Just try to resist the fried confections called Elephant Ears, or Funnel Cakes, hot and white with dusted confectioner's sugar. Move on, there's still more to tempt the tastebuds — cotton candy, and taffy — pulled, cut, and wrapped, right before your eyes.

For a quarter, relax on open-sided tractor-pulled cars as they pick up or drop off visitors, around the Fairgrounds. Step off, as the loudspeaker announces the Natural Resources Building. Walk over, then, to the Pioneer Village. Pay, to step beyond the canvas walls separating the nonpaying crowd from the customers, at the tractor pull. The roar of hundred-thousand-dollar machines still ringing in your ears, walk away, past a clutter of booths selling leather belts, helium balloons, or personalized license plates. Pick up a free litter bag, at a radio station's mobile van.

Enjoy people watching. Nowhere else does a group dress so uniquely for an event. First, there's the rodeo crowd, identified by their black-and-white plastic-lace cowboy hats with feather bands. They wear black shirts tucked in skin-tight jeans, and cowboy boots that click on the sidewalk as they walk. The ladies are thin, their men — big bears.

Oh yes, the farm crowd: serviceable jeans, checkered or plaid shirts or well-washed tees, straw hats, or fraying logo-brimmed caps — advertising beer, farm equipment, or hybrid seeds. The women are plump, stuffed in polyester slacks, grinning in permanent crinkly smiles. The men are sun-aged, sinewy, built for chores. The teens are anxious-eyed, their 4-H calf not yet judged or sold for slaughter.

The city crowd, in different sizes, shapes, and dress of their own, smell of sunscreen lotion or summer perfume. Tropical print dresses, canvas baby-equipment bags, and strollers announce moms. Teens in black tee shirts with fluorescent rock-group logos silk-screened on front and back, retirees holding hands, strolling slowly into the quilt exhibits, or moving past displays of pumpkins, tomatoes, and jam.

We're all there; meet me at the grandstand at five o'clock.

☆❤☆

THESE NEWFANGLED INVENTIONS

☆♥☆

Laura,
seat 13D in the airplane
taking her home to Minnesota
for Thanksgiving, smiled as I sat down next to her. As the plane lifted off from Seattle, we fell into easy conversation — soon getting around to: "and what do *you* do?"

In her mid-twenties, Laura believes she is part of the new wave; she knows she is "an individual with a lot of talents and much to give, but I haven't quite figured out how my gifts are to be shared to make the world a better place."

Laura settles back, smiles, and continues: "Instead of the traditional decade at one company, climbing the corporate ladder...I don't see this as a reality anymore, only for the select few...I work at lots of different places, meet many people, and learn — I think — much more about life."

She grabbed the grocery-sack-brown placemat from the tray of our pathetic "in-flight snack," and wrote down some more thoughts, interested now in my quest for "hugs and hopes."

"I know the information superhighway is such a buzzword these days, but I think it is a part of something much bigger for this past century. And that something is the incredible leaps society has made in communication.

"From the telegraph and horseback days to paying a utility bill from your home computer, I think these technologies have really brought our world together. We understand each other (different countries,...cultures) a little better.

"Just by seeing other parts of the world on TV, it brings a better understanding and accepting. Not to mention travel, experiencing cultures first hand.

"Well, I hope I'm not too cliche, but it boggles my mind how far we've come and the potential we have yet to be."

☆❤☆

> *1943 —*
> *The first*
> *computer —*
> *the IBM Mark I,*
> *(the Automatic*
> *Sequence Controlled*
> *Calculator) —*
> *developed by*
> *Howard Aiken,*
> *was tested.*

☆♥☆

We were glad Laura took the time to share, thanked her, and settled back to buckle up for our plane's descent. Then we noticed a smile from
>the white-haired,
>wire-rim-bespectacled
>lady, seated to
>Laura's right.

"What have you two been talking about?" she quizzed. Ah, *she* knew what to treasure, from this century:

"I've recently retired from a job that, well, there was a *lot* of deadlines — a lot of stress. I used to say, 'I just *hate* Henry Ford and his darned internal combustion engine! Just give me a pony and a satchel for my papers, and I'll take 'em home!'"

Big grin; pulling her red sweater tighter around her, hugging her own wisdom, she added:

"I just hope we don't fall for all that stuff, and think technology is *better*. Some [here, she made quotation marks in the air with her fingers] 'advances in communication' — she paused, for effect — *separate* us. We need *contact*!"

☆♥☆

☆♥☆

Two of our respondents, living far across the continent from each other, both believe the amazing advances of this century came about because of World War II.

Bob,
an antique store owner,
in Georgetown, Texas,
feels the "World War II situation was very important; it changed everything — technology, *and* our viewpoint. I felt an excitement after the war, in everyone. It's new times. People were empowered to follow their own dreams."

Bob is even hopeful that technology may bring a solution to the problem of, as he calls it, "the ad age, the age of hype." He is afraid we've gone a little overboard, advertising that just because we say so, . . . "it must be true."

But, after all, we *are* finding a way to live with technology; Bob knows we'll work it out.

> *Richard, deli owner in Austin, TX, remembers "traveling everywhere" on a free railroad pass. "We didn't pay a dime." The son of a freight office attendant, Richard hopes "railroads become a major source of transportation, again."*

☆♥☆

☆♥☆

Ivan,
a Bulgarian physicist,
working in Vancouver,
British Columbia,
thought very carefully about what he wanted to say.

We had met, years ago, on the campus of the University of British Columbia; Ivan is part of a large group of researchers working at TRIUMF (TriUniversity Meson Facility). There the world's largest particle accelerator offers hope in cancer treatment advances, as well as in the basic field of energy. Tiny stuff is very big, at this turn of the century.

> 1928 — Adm. Richard E. Byrd's first Antarctic expedition.

> 1989 — The Berlin Wall came down.

Ivan wrote down what he wants us to remember, and cherish:

"The end of World War II, and the following 'Wind of Freedom' — national, political...the expression and exchange of information,...the freedom of travel. The atomic [nuclear] energy release, and the computer's invention and implementation in everyday life, including the ease of knowledge receiving."

Proud of his Eastern European heritage, Ivan remembers one more thing to be proud of: "the first Sputnik launch."

> Space exploration is a milestone in this century. Barb, Bill, and Leonard, relaxing at Saranac Lake, NY, agree,"This is the century we escaped the bonds of earth! This is the century of great technology."

71

☆♥☆

Merrill, a court officer in Georgetown, Texas, smiles, lays down her pen, glances at the phone, and adds a vote for computers. "I used to have to go pull a file; now, I just flip it up on a screen!"

The phone rings again; it's the fax they've been waiting for — she alerts the judge. Free for another moment, Merrill adds to her list:

> May 9, 1960 — The FDA approved the use of "The Pill" as a method of birth control.

"disposable diapers! disposable *bottles*!" We laugh, and agree, "we've come a *long* way."

Merrill must now reply to the fax, technology simplifying her day.

☆♥☆

☆❤☆

Most of us could list ten things that did not exist before this century. And, all our lists would be different.
        Mabel,
           my college roommate's mother,
           now ninety-three-years-old,
says "every farmer I ever knew had a cow named Mabel."

She remembers *her* father, a man who "was always inventing creature-comforts." Oh, how Mabel wishes — giggling — "if *only* he could have seen a *car wash!*"

☆❤☆

What would be on your list?

☆♥☆

Since I shop European-style, walking to neighborhood stores, I see Mark almost daily. Young, sincere, and always helpful, he makes sure the courtesy coffeepot is full, the fresh flowers are watered, the vegetables trimmed. "May I weigh that for you?" accompanies his ever-ready smile.

  Mark,
    supermarket produce clerk,
    in Indianapolis, Indiana,
asked what I was writing; he became excited, about what he might contribute. Television won, hands down. He said he'd make a few notes. Soon, he had a notebook page filled, folded into a pocket-sized square, waiting for my next trip to the store.

  Mark remembers how, in 1976, the gymnast Nadia Comaneci "entered our living rooms and our hearts through our TV screens," changing our opinion of "an abstract enemy — the communists."

  Through TV, Mark suggests, "our natural borders and cultural divisions become less important. TV tends to emphasize what is *common* to the human condition."

  He goes on: TV coverage of the Midwest flood of '93 brought us "real, actual, people to whom many of us were inspired to help, through Red Cross donations. TV personalizes the victories of a Michael Jordan, or a cancer survivor. The laughter provided by an evening of sitcoms is a tonic for the spirit."

Mark knows, of course, TV can sensationalize "the negative, leaving many people feeling that the world is mostly a bad place."

"I hope," he concludes, "TV will work harder to 'sensationalize' the good."

☆♥☆

OUR HEROES

☆♥☆

Richard,
the deli owner,
in Austin, Texas,
erases yesterday's soup specials from the chalk board, puts up "potato cheddar" and "Southwest bean," wipes off the ice-cream-parlor table tops, and then pauses for a sip of coffee.

"I've *always* treasured freedom, and *responsibility*. I *love* what happened in the Sixties!" Richard feels guilty, that he's "apolitical." "Right now, I feel no matter what you try to do, no matter who you put in office, it'll turn out the same.

"But I still have my heroes! — Churchill, LBJ, Gandhi. But you know — who are my daughter's heroes? I'm *not* one who wants the 'good old days' back (we didn't have penicillin), you know?"

"I read in the newspaper, the other day, a man said he sees a lotta *adults* around here. But where are the *grown-ups*?" Richard roars, at his own comment.

> 1901 —
> *The first Nobel Prizes were awarded.*
> *In physics, W.C. Roentgen won, for the discovery of x-ray.*

Watching Her Halo Slip

When I was six, and worshiped mother
I couldn't believe she was ever six,
or worshiped hers.
But she told me so;
she told me of a luncheon,
    perfect table
    gleaming silver
    roses in a cut-glass bowl.
Elizabeth was allowed
to meet the ladies in the parlor;
Huldah had taught her how
to greet a guest.
Elizabeth was allowed
to carry plates to tables;
Huldah, herself,
would do the rest.
Returning to the kitchen,
Elizabeth watched her.
Watched in horror;
fish-shaped mousse, newly spawned
from copper mold flipped wildly to the floor.
Quickly ssshhhhing daughter,
Huldah acted.
Grabbing spoon and dish, she knelt
to save the day.
The ladies of Des Moines
ate salmon;
stern look
reminding Elizabeth
what she dare not
say.

Did you dream about a hero, when you were a child? Who is your hero now?

☆♥☆

Kwaduo,
the journalism professor
from Ghana, East Africa,
stepped out of his apartment just as I was unlocking my door. We exchanged the usual greetings, exclaimed our dismay over the day's awful news. Kwaduo pursed his lips, rolled his eyes, and muttered:

"We need new *heroes*; and heroines!"

I agreed. It came to me later; that evening, as I wrote in my journal, I pondered the absence of heroes:

"We should find a mother who reads books to her toddler, find a father who shows seven hyper nine-year-olds how to hammer a nail — 'Well now, son, I don't think I'd put my finger *there*.' We should cherish the neighbor who teaches you how to get to the recycling center, the one who shares homemade bread. Perhaps our role models for tomorrow are next door."

The next morning, I knocked at Kwaduo's apartment. "Got a minute?" I showed him what I'd written.

A big grin spread, over the whitest teeth you've ever seen: "*Yes*! *That's* what I mean!"

☆♥☆

☆♥☆

We won! We won!

It's one of those winter Saturdays, gray snow wisps along the driveway, five kids in the house, and more bills than money. But tonight, yes, tonight, there's a Pacers game on TV. Mike and Nancy and their kids are coming over, and we'll order a pizza.

And in that gathering, watching million-dollar basketball players achieve another amazing slam dunk or rebound, we win.

Everyone leaping off the couches, chairs, and floor pillows, everyone laughing and screaming: "Yes! Yes! We did it!" We won. No, they won; but for a brief moment, the bills are forgotten, you don't have to go to work tomorrow, and the victory is sweet.

☆♥☆

*August 28, 1945 —
Branch Richey signs
Jackie Robinson to
play for the
Brooklyn Dodgers.
Salary — $600/month,
signing bonus of
$3500.*

WE'RE PASSIONATE ABOUT LIFE

☆♥☆

As well as heroes, my neighbor once said, we need passions: "You know, something you LOVE to do."
    Bob,
        the antique store owner,
            in Georgetown, Texas,
had made his passion his business. His love of antiques, his belief that every object has "the charm of the human side. Who made it? Who used it? Why did they use it, instead of something else?"

It was an unusually warm day for Texas in January; the doors to Bob's shop were thrown open. Next door, in his wife's garden shop, we sat in old wooden children's chairs by the electric fireplace, sipping coffee.

Bob was bewildered, his weathered face crinkled: Why would *anyone* want to go to a mall?"

Bob rose, to return to his own shop; a customer had inquired about fountain pens. They were in the glass display case; once, someone's treasure — about to find new hands. Bob would help.

Grandma In The Gift Shop

Fluttering among soft folds of silk,
delicate fingers
take inventory of her bodice.
Antique brooches in the showcase
bring smiles —
memories to her of jewelry
she once wore
at the throat she now taps.
Glitter of jewels in the case
leaps, to ignite
her eyes.
Gaze wanders;
"What's his name?"
she asks, finding the porcelain figure.
Lifted down from the shelf,
placed on velvet before her,
now she can stroke Oriental robes,
trace long creamy beard,
nudge his wrinkled forehead.
Raising delicate eyelids,
she repeats politely,
"Do you know what his name is?"
"Longevity" is found on the
price tag.

She smiles,
and greets him properly.
Cradling him in her hand,
she ignores friends pleas to
"C'mon!"
She tells of moving soon
to Florida.
"He should go with me,
I think."
Fourteen ninety-five
ransoms her new friend;
Longevity leaves together.

> "What all this means, of course, is that I rely on objects not only as reservoirs of the past but also as promises of an open-ended future — a future that might, at any point, circle back into a past in which I take up bicycle riding again and kiss Chris Dybdahl or make collages or discourse impressively on economics."
> — Noelle Oxenhandler

☆❤☆

Think about an heirloom you treasure:

For many, the quest of finding bargains at a flea-market, church rummage sale, or spread out on a neighborhood yard, stirs the heart. "Treasures!" my daughter calls them; "wonderful things we *need*!" Yup — she's my daughter.

In 1991, I wrote in my journal:

"I admit, I am a garage-sale junkie. I have bought five-dozen pairs of enameled copper cuff links, because they were such a bargain. I have carried home a child's maple rocking chair, balancing it upside-down on my head. If there's a cardboard sign on a telephone pole, I cross the street to see where and when the sale will be held. Balloons spotted a block away lure me off my intended walking path.

"The possibility that someone else might get the beads I should have can make my pulse race. How can I get to all the sales first?

"You begin to recognize other garage-sale junkies; the worst time to see one walking fast, clutching a filled grocery sack and a dog bed, is when they are coming down the steep driveway, as you are going up.

"They beat you. Lose one turn; start over."

☆♥☆

What is your passion?

— For Carole, it's dancing. She has been known to go out-of-state, for the evening, to Contra dance. Carole fondly remembers the dance in Kansas; fiddles chasing notes through the timbers of the barn that once belonged to her grandfather.

— For David, it's his garden. He's built platform boxes for the vegetables, pored over catalogs of the year's newest offers, hovered over emerging beans, as if coaxing them would urge them higher on the strings.

— Camilla runs. And runs off the tightness accumulated from a high-stress job. "I *love* jogging along the canal, behind Butler University, where you can see the river, beyond. I love running under a Spring canopy of newly leaved trees."

— My sister, Barb, cherishes family photos, squares of crochet-work our grandmother once made; Barb has them framed. She is the one to keep in touch with everyone, telling me on the phone how Bonner and Febe are doing, or "so-and-so" sends their love. Ancestors and connected friends; Barb savors family ties.

— For Mary Lee, it has to be mugs and mugs

of coffee. "Everyone *knows* not to ask me anything before I've had my first cup of the day," she laughs. Of course, those mugs of coffee taste better, if she and Harry are out in the Blue Ridge Mountains, camping.

☆❤☆

☆♥☆

The crowd was waiting for the mayor to arrive. Balloons decorated the tops of fence posts, someone began setting up a microphone, and children tried out the new playground. It was a very happy day. Not long ago, a child had died on that corner, struck down by a speeding car. Today, we gathered to commemorate a park in her honor. A park the city, a handful of businesses and a lot of helping neighbors built together.

>Carole,

>who loves dancing,

>looked around the street.

We had been reminiscing. We were talking about the good things in life, the little passions like dancing, that keep us going. "You know," she suddenly offered, "you have to have passion before com-passion!" Carole pronounced it as two words, for emphasis. "*Com*-passion," she repeated. "Caring for others, helping out." We nodded, in agreement.

"When you are *full*, then you can *give!*" Carole grinned: "It's like that oxygen mask on airplanes. You know, they tell you to do your own first, and then you can help others!"

☆♥☆

*Picnics, old movies,
working on a classic car...
What is the oxygen that fills your soul?*

HONEST HARD WORK

☆❤☆

More treasured than overcoats, gold cufflinks, or the blue-flowered dishes, our parents handed down a way of life. These values were mentioned more often than any other topic, by those who replied for this book.

Ruth,
a seventy-eight-year-old
mall-walker,
in Bellevue, Washington,
remembers: "My husband 'n I *never* knew from his 'n hers — it was *always* together!"

Ruth met her husband Adolf at a dance. "He was a *gentleman.*" He had come from Berlin in 1939; they married in 1941. She adds, "When we were first married, we *lived* with my *parents!*"

Ruth sips ice water with a slice of lemon in it, slowly. She savors her memories, shares them with the walkers gathering for "coffee after."

"Now *his* parents were from Russia. They had a huge tobacco farm there. Oh yes, and *my* mother had to go out in the *hall*, to let in the iceman!"

"You know, we had such *freedom* then. We could flirt, and nothing came of it; we had such *wholesome innocence.*"

☆❤☆

> *Barb, Bill and Leonard, chatting one day at Saranac Lake, NY, agreed, "The Fifties were good years. The War was over; people were happy. It was such a time of innocence and optimism!"*

☆♥☆

Harold,
a house-painter
from Pageland, South Carolina, sat next to me on the Greyhound bus from Charlotte, North Carolina, to Knoxville, Tennessee. Lean, trim, and scrubbed fresh, Harold wore jeans, and a white tee shirt with "paintbrush swipes" of vivid red, purple, green, and blue. "U-M," it spelled, on his front; "B-R-O," on the back. Harold was on his way to visit his sister, in Colorado, the one who "works at the casino."

Harold guesses, in the future, family will "probably be broken down more." He reflects slowly, decides, and answers my questions.

"My parents *both* taught me *to work hard* and *to value education.*" Harold has a grown son and daughter, and hopes he has passed these lessons on.

> Donna, nurse for an inner-city program, in a downtown church in Charlotte, NC hugs "the gift of presence. Being present to ourselves, to others . . . being really there." Donna hopes we grow to be in tune with "what's gonna work the best for all."

The future? "Family will change," he thinks; "we're gonna *have* to make larger groups of people together. Everybody realize, we should treat each other *all the same.*"

It will take hard work, he thinks, but we can do it.

☆♥☆

The Starspeck Question

The three-year-old asks: "What do?"
That's a good question.
How do we answer for the day,
muddled around in,
in our grown-up way?
Did we launch a smile,
   plant a kiss,
      dare to miss
an hour in front of a flickering
          screen?
The baby twins, each in a different
         way,
ask what we're doing,
what we have to say.
Mister pokey-finger
jabs and prods, investigating,
instigating;
Missy flapper-hands
unhinges her tiny butterflies
before your eyes
asking the same.
"What do?"
Are you part of the solution?
Please?

☆♥☆

Seeking Wisdom

☆❤☆

I got off the elevator at the seventh floor, in the tall building on the north edge of the University of Texas campus, in Austin, hoping I'd found the right office. "Come in!" He bows, Japanese manners gracious, in the Physics Department cramped office. One desk, one chair available for a visitor, stacks and stacks of charts and papers. I am aware of the foreign language of pure numbers crawling all over a wall-sized blackboard to the left.

>Tomio Petrosky,
>for twenty years, co-worker
>with Nobel laureate
>Ilya Prigogine,
>on Chaos Theory,

offers some of his time, a lot of his wisdom.

"Science *must* use philosophy to find the question," he offers. "But it is *not* a mutual relation[ship]. If philosophy wants to find the *answer* ... must come to science!"

For twenty years, these men have been refining their proof of Professor Prigogine's theory. "The unique ingredient of chaos," says Petrosky, "is *instability*."

He explains, by suggesting that western civilization, art, music, all have "an interesting tension...conflict, unresolved. This leads to quite unstable [sic]." Languages compete; he who thinks in numbers, sometimes in Japanese, is trying to communicate with a poet, in English. "*In*stability," he corrects himself. "Now you take China: Chang Dynasty introduced *stability*. For 2000 years now, nothing happens!"

Petrosky is emphatic: "Instability leads to change. That is my understanding. At the very unstable moment, you have a surprise!" He beams, rolling back in his chair in laughter.

We talked about students, about learning, about youth. "What means is young?" he asks. And quickly provides his own answer: "Means open the brain!" More laughs, as he checks my eyes, to be sure I understand.

> *In 1938, Teflon was accidentally discovered by DuPont chemist Roy Plunkett, while working on refrigerants.*

Petrosky is frustrated with the student who methodically follows all the rules, proves his case.

"I *hate* 'zero,' 'one,' 'black,' 'white'...nature is more rich! We need, sometimes, to ignore the rule!"

What does he like, then, in a student, I ask? "Surprises!" he grins back. "My dream for the coming century is that the young *participate* in creativity."

☆♥☆

Practice looking for surprises. A phone call that changes things, a book that falls off a shelf at your feet, the weather cancels your picnic. Ah, but then...

☆♥☆

Paula,
"Keeper of Old Things for a lineal Native American tradition," wonderer about life, now lives in SanAnselmo, California.

Paula's prose is a treasure, itself. Listen to the flow of her words:

"All Life is a Learning. What we learn in this Life goes with us when we make the Great Return — our gift for the gift of this Life. So whatever happens to the Human Beings in the long run, we will have made our contribution to Universe.

> *"Life is a succession of lessons which must be lived to be understood."*
> —Helen Keller

"Remember the Learning. Remember the joy of sunset and sunrise, the fragrance of new-mown grass, the soft sound of life new-born.

"Sometimes wisdom only comes after great foolishness. I hope that the great foolishness of our near-destruction of Earth's ability to sustain present life leads to the wisdom we will need to assist her healing.

"From this century I cherish our painful wisdom in effectively opposing the spread of totalitarian governance. I cherish our wisdom in rebuilding Europe and Japan after WWII. I cherish the way each generation must relearn the ways of self-governance. I cherish our wisdom in beginning physical exploration of the moon. I cherish all the many learnings!

"May they benefit us in the future! They were painfully earned.

"If our children, and after them their children, remember our many learnings, their wisdom will be greater than ours. We will have prepared the seedbed which they will then harvest.

"Let it be so."

☆♥☆

> *John, of Indianapolis, hopes "We can learn to dance together." He remembers a grandmother "who had soft arms for hugging" and taught him the "difference between education and wisdom."*

☆♥☆

Liz,
gentle guide, and therapist,
in Austin, Texas,
remembers that her family always encouraged *"knowledge."* She stresses, "all sorts of *learning.*" They taught me that we are part of the larger community; there's some strand, some tie.

"I always treasured learning about all types of people, all kinds of situations. Getting to know one another, Liz feels, is how we "find out we are connected."

☆♥☆

Who is the most recent person you've gotten to know?

☆♥☆

Andy Jacobs, Jr., long-term U.S. Representative, 10th District, Indiana, believes "The future will be bright or bleak to the degree to which our society decides to accomplish universal education, especially cognitive preschool for the educationally disadvantaged. The latter, I think, could make impersonal violent street crime almost obsolete within fifteen or twenty years into the new century. And then the high road of that future would be marvelous for all of our children's children and their children too."

☆♥☆

☆♥☆

Hal,
a global thinker,
living in Austin, Texas,
suggests where we find our strength, in the century ahead:

"It seems to me that the single most likely reason for America's economic, military and political success during this century, the most plausible source of its ability to become a superpower, has been our open, mass education system, including free education through high school.

"During the next century, I hope our country will extend free education through the highest university levels to all qualified students. This seems a natural upgrading of our major source of strength."

☆♥☆

VOLUNTEER TO GET IT DONE

☆♥☆

This was the century we stepped up, stepped out, joined in, and faced the task.
>Mitzi,
>>my college roomate,
>>now living in
>>Savannah, Georgia,

celebrates "Hugs for those who took the risks, fought the wars, flew the rockets, created the inventions and kept us going. They brought us through the Depression, Polio, World Wars, loss of leaders, and perils of wind and weather."

☆♥☆

☆♥☆

Liz,
the Baby-boom era
"self-admitted weird person
in camouflage,"
now a family therapist,
in Kerrville, Texas,
carries a leather briefcase, wears the professional suit, but remains a pioneer spirit.

Liz thinks we "began the brashness of a whole new age," fresh, eager to learn, to try new things, "surviving after a huge war, with *hope*."

Liz radiates, when she describes what she sees as our future:

"The young, today, are exciting! They're more *questing* as a group, than I was, at that age. We're finding out how we're connected; most people see some strand, some tie."

Liz sips her coffee, waits a moment, then adds: "I hope we have the courage to follow the strengths that are already developing."

☆♥☆

☆♥☆

We sat in her office, one January morn, close to the space heater beneath her desk, warming our hands on mugs of coffee. Amid the herbs, pottery, braided soft leather and trinket necklaces, and — over there — a packet of Texas Bluebonnet seeds, we talked.

>Judy,
>garden and gift shop owner,
>editor, author of a book on
>computer networking,
>lives in Georgetown, Texas.

She leans back; *way* back, as her swivel-chair tips: "I remember," pulling herself upright again, "when Betty Friedan came to my college!" Checking her computer screen, Judy continues:

"This probably made more difference in my life than anything. The history is long; well, it didn't affect my mother, but it *did me!*"

June 3, 1900 — Cloakworkers founded the International Ladies Garment Workers Union, in New York City. They held their meetings in a Lower East Side hall.

Judy smiles: "I came from a *very* traditional household. Women didn't make decisions." She glances over, to emphasize her point: "openly!"

"And then I learned," she laughs, "you *could* do it! And right up *front!*"

☆♥☆

☆♥☆

I remember Shirley as the little pixie of the neighborhood, the friend of my younger sister, Barb. Visiting my sister a few years ago, Shirley and I reconnected.

>Shirley,
>now interested in
>metaphysics and Tai Chi,
>resides in Potomac, Maryland.

I just know she'd love to sit over a cup of tea in Judy's shop, poking around a little; an herb here, a computer trick there, and the warmth of a kindred spirit.

From Maryland, Shirley writes: "I will cherish the nearly century-long struggle and attainment and continuing process of establishing the rights of women: to vote, to gain recognition, to be employed in any occupation, to raise families, to love and cherish other women — as friends or as mates."

Shirley continues: "...to become elected leaders, to gain equal pay for equal work, to be educated and taught in the same manner and encouraged in the same subjects as male students, and many more successes women can celebrate."

☆♥☆

★♥★

Billy Rae Stubblefield, a general jurisdiction judge presiding in Georgetown, Texas, stood, to greet me, welcoming this writer into his paneled office. Gracious, trim and handsome, with a genial smile, the judge settled back into his leather chair. He swiveled, to face my question:

"I feel it has something to do with the struggle for progress, that carries with it an optimism ... courage ... dogged determination of the human spirit that made the march of progress possible."

The judge thought a moment, chose his words, and continued:

"Instead of [believing] we've sown the seeds of our own destruction, we have to look at individual cases." Judge Stubblefield moved forward, elbows on his desk, to cite an example, "We no longer, in this country, at least, lynch people on a regular basis. We did, in 1900!"

Leaning back again, gazing upward in reflection, he went on, "As human beings, we have to look at our achievements, to draw strength from them, so we have the courage to carry on."

The busy judge had time for one more comment. He hopes, he added, "we have the good sense to take our own destinies in our own hands." He concludes, "and that our institutions — and that's *all* our institutions! — political, religious, educational — continue to be responsible to the will of the people."

☆♥☆

WITH LIBERTY AND JUSTICE FOR ALL
☆♥☆

Hands over hearts, we stand to pledge: "...with liberty, and justice for all." It's been a struggle, to make that promise a reality. The good news is that we might actually be getting somewhere, according to
Phil Bremen,
a former TV anchor/reporter,
now Press Secretary for
Frank O'Bannon, Governor
of the State of Indiana.

Phil has the TV anchor's rugged good looks, the resonant voice, and an extra sparkle appears in his eye, when he talks about the future.

"I wasn't around for the first half of this century," he admits, "but what seems most impressive to me about the second half, is the barriers that once separated people and now have fallen. I don't mean the barriers of time and space — barriers shrunk by superhighways and jetliners, television towers and satellites, cellular phones and computers, impressive as they all are.

"No, the fallen barriers I find most striking are those of attitude and ideology. Barriers that kept peoples enslaved; barriers that withheld education, accommodations, and work on the basis of gender, ethnicity, or disability. Barriers of callousness and ignorance that condemned one generation after another to abuse and shame."

Phil continues, "All the work is not done; for all the progress that has been made, of course, many of those barriers are still standing. Let's not forget barriers of opportunity that keep so many people — even in rich lands — from enjoying good health and greater fulfillment."

"Barriers dividing us and people like us (whoever we may be) from everyone else," Phil concludes: "In the coming century, I yearn to see those barriers crumble into dust."

☆♥☆

> *In 1900, requests went out to over 3000 patent attorneys, newspaper editors, and manufacturers, seeking black inventors. The U.S. Commission to the Paris Exposition of 1900 featured, in the U.S. exhibit, a display featuring 350 "new patents granted to black inventors."*

☆♥☆

Judy,
in her office in the
garden/gift shop in Texas,
hopes "people will regain generosity of spirit, and be less quick to judge." Judy hopes she can pass down to her grandchildren the practice of establishing connections "to each other, to all of nature, and our Earth."

☆♥☆

Laura,
the young seatmate
in the plane over Minnesota,
wrote on the placemat:
"I would like our children's children to continue keeping their minds open to accepting people that are different from themselves. It's what we, as humans, are about — relating with our peers. And in my Christian view, life and death are about every human being one and the same."

☆♥☆

☆♥☆

And remember Vic,
the condo doorman
in Austin?

Vic is positive that "the main thing is getting along with your neighbor." He adds, "Disregard color, pull together. Like a big puzzle ... you know, if there's a part missing, you can't see the picture."

☆♥☆

> *Tammy, a college student and cheerleader, in Kerrville, TX, wants "The children of the future to know that each little step they choose to take in their lives has a tremendous impact on the world."*

✮ ❤ ✮

What it will take is optimism, and hard work. Meet both:

    Charles,
    now a hotel security officer,
    retired from a career as a
    mechanical engineer,

sat in the Holiday Inn lobby, downtown Charlotte, North Carolina. A smile in my direction, and I moved coat, coffee, and notebook to the chair nearest his stool; Charles would be fun to get to know.

"I'm a *very* positive person," he began. "I believe the greatest thing this century has shown is *change*. For the *better*! Number one, racial. Why, I remember, as a boy in New York City, segregation. And then in the Armed Forces. And, here in the South. But we *are* changing!"

"Number two," he counted off, "attitude toward women. It's so obvious! Changing *every* day! Why, look at the Packwood case!"

Charles had more, to illustrate the changes we can be proud of: "My mother is ninety-seven. English. Actually," he pauses briefly, shocked at his own realization, "she's quite negative. When she starts talking about child abuse on TV, I just say, 'Do you realize, early in this century, when you could buy and sell a child on your streets of London, and *no one* knew, or cared?' We *are* changing," Charles finished, with a huge grin.

☆♥☆

Where do you see change for the better?

☆♥☆

Hal, who served
during World War II
as a bomber pilot,
is retired now, and living in
Austin, Texas.

We had met, four years ago. Imagine our surprise to reconnect at a condo swimming pool. Yes, he would give some thought to this century issue; we set a time to get together later.

Hal had given it a lot of thought. When I was welcomed into his home, he had a prepared response typed and lying on his desk. This community of peace that so many speak of goes global for Hal:

In a "Memorandum About Your Turn-of-the-Century Questions," he writes:

"During this century the apparent human condition of willingness to resort to maximum uses of force in warfare to resolve disputes between coequal political groups (an average of three wars per year for the past 1000 years) resulted in actual unprecedented, massive destruction and human suffering. Advances in technology have made these extremes in terror possible, so possible that we only narrowly escaped risking an atomic war which had the capability of destroying all of human life.

"In the next century, it is my hope that the nations of the world will find a way to transfer to the United Nations sole authority to have and use international force, i.e. international disputes will come under law."

Working together, he sees as our only way.

☆♥☆

☆♥☆

After I read Hal's offering, during which time his wife Carlie came back and forth from the kitchen with homemade olive bread, a vegetable pâté, and some wine, we settled in the living room to talk.
    Carlie,
        energetic civic volunteer
      there in Austin,
is specific about her response: "our *beginnings* of the end of racial prejudice!" Carlie dearly hopes "we *complete* that end "

Just as quickly as she served more pâté, Carlie asked: "How do you feel about the 'Million Man March'? It was *marvelous!*" she answered herself. "To make the men responsible to the family, and responsible to the *greater* family, which is *nation!*"

Carlie had a lot to add: "The Voting Rights Act of 1965..." She waited, while I said yes, I'd been hearing that, from others. Carlie nodded: "It virtually eliminated *any* qualifications!" Thinking a moment, which gave me a chance to spread some more pâté on another wedge of her delicious bread, Carlie reminisced about Martin Luther King.

"He was the breakthrough! Both peaceful *and*

non-violent! We learned so much. And I believe he was the impetus for his people, the belief in working together. He instilled *pride!*"

We talked of city government, downtown malls, and public transportation. Then Carlie had one more hope to add: "I hope the *media* will assume a more moral and ethical response to their information gathering . . . and distribution." She paused. "It's just about the *ethics* of it."

☆♥☆

> *Matthew, Maurice, and Martin Bucksbaum built the first shopping center of our century in 1956, naming it the Town and Country in Cedar Rapids, Iowa.*

⭐❤️⭐

Think back, or ask Grandma. Do you remember, before November 11th became known as "Veteran's Day," when it was called "Armistice Day"? As a child did you decorate your bike with red, white, and blue streamers, or march, carrying a toy drum, in the children's parade around your block?

Celebrating the end of World War I was a very exciting day in 1918. Parade in your heart, with those first children, urged to bang away on a dishpan with a wooden spoon, or shout at the top of their lungs: "The war is *over!* Hooray!"

I came along later, as a child of World War II. Imagine our amazement, after ration books, too little butter or meat, dark evenings during "air-raid drills," to hear the grownups chatter and spread the news — "It's over!" Children, the war is over, let's have a parade. And we did.

> *1949 —*
> *Harry S. Truman signed a joint resolution of Congress act, declaring June 14th to be known henceforth as "Flag Day."*

A few found small flags to carry, some had a drum or toy horn, but most of all, I remember the joy on our parents' faces. Gee, we were having all the fun, but *they* were so happy. Hooray!

⭐❤️⭐

Remember To Vote

☆♥☆

Election day, 1995,
brought few to the polls
at our fire station.
    Little to vote for this time, many folks thought; and anyway, why bother? But look closely, at those who do come. Over there, signing in at the clerk's book — the older woman, dressed all in red, white and blue: white jacket, blue trim, blue slacks and sweatshirt, with a red and white scarf. Even her earrings were blue. A walking vote, for our country, and the privilege of casting her ballot.

☆♥☆

Very few voters came in,
all afternoon.
The clerks played solitaire,
one read David Copperfield.
    Even the faded silk flag, in the corner of the community room, leaned against the wall. Outside, the

sound of tires on gravel. A voter is coming! Books and papers disappeared, smiles came back: "This way, sir!"

He voted; we talked. It was simple, he told me — "I gotta do my duty!" His eyes said, "Who wouldn't?"

> *Don, precinct committeeman, at the polls November, 1995, in Indianapolis, reflected on community. Don recalls concerts in the park, neighbors sitting on front porches. "I think," he says, "people are the same.* ***Good*** *people are still good people."*

☆♥☆

Betty came to vote, and heard us talking.

"Why, when I was young," she chimed in, "we even had *parades*. We'd have torchlight gatherings, speeches, everything! And later, as the women counted the votes, why, people would stand around outside the windows and cheer when they heard the name called out."

> *On August 26, 1920, the 19th Amendment gave women the right to vote.*

☆♥☆

Andy Jacobs, Jr.,
long-term U.S.Representative,
10th District, Indiana,
retired in 1996 after more than a quarter-century of service to our country. He replied to my questions, by letter:

"I believe that for Americans the 1965 Voting Rights Act might prove to be of the greatest value to our society in terms of 20th Century accomplishments.

"The Voting Rights Act in 1965 ended our Nation's embarrassing hypocrisy of denying the right to vote even to some of those who had faced death on battlefields to save our country. With the enactment of that law we took a giant stride toward achieving those beautiful words, 'liberty and justice for all.'"

That left me with a quest: look up the Voting Rights Act of 1965. I asked here and there, but no one I talked with remembered, any better than I did, what it covered. A month or so went by, with it still on my "To Do" list.

☆♥☆

★ ❤ ★

It was a blustery January day, in Austin, Texas, when I walked over to the LBJ Museum and Library, on the edge of the University of Texas campus. Ask, follow the guide map, go around the circle...there it is! Where, better, would I ever find out about the 1965 Voting Rights Act; it had been enacted under Johnson. I walked faster than the Texas wind whipping my coat. I was on a mission.

"Excuse me, please, could you help me? I am looking for information," I asked. "Could I please step *behind* those ropes, to take notes? Oh, thank you!"

On the wall, framed and glass-protected, there it was...right in the main lobby. The left end of the display case contained a black-and-white poster of some children on playground swings; red letters over their black arms and legs urged "Push me, mister...register and vote." "NAACP" at the bottom indicated who had published the poster.

Move to the right; there it is, a full copy of the actual two pages of legislation. The display card informed:

"August 6, 1965 Lyndon Baines Johnson signs into law The Voting Rights Act of '65, ...which...suspends the use of literacy tests and eliminates other qualifying measures used to deny anyone the right to vote...also authorizes the federal government to appoint voting examiners to supervise...."

I was shifting to read the telegrams of celebration and the quote "While many citizens were elated, there are those..." when I sensed the flurry of guards, media, and action behind me. I turned, just as the mahogany casket bearing Barbara Jordan was wheeled by my coat.

☆♥☆

☆♥☆

Suddenly I remembered the headlines of the day — Barbara Jordan had died the day before; her body would lie in state for twenty-four hours, in the LBJ Museum. Barbara Jordan; University of Texas law professor, and former U.S. Representative. Barbara Jordan, national hero; now I remembered the flags at half-staff around campus, the sadness in the chill air.

They rushed the casket out of sight; media followed. Stating my name to a guard, and my meager freelance association with an Indianapolis newspaper, I suddenly found myself walking in with the media. We arrived upstairs, an hour before the public would be allowed in; silence wrapped crews and cameramen, respect and awe held sway.

We milled about, seeking quotes, checking details. Yes, the curved staircase is Italian travertine marble; the obelisk behind her casket, "We call it the pilon," is black granite. Four LBJ quotes, one on each side; I was strongly taken by the appropriateness of the one on the far side from where Jordan's casket lay:

"Until justice is blind to color, until education is unaware of race, until opportunity is unconcerned with the color of men's skins, emancipation will be a proclamation but not a fact."

"Over there," someone whispered; "I think it's her." A dignified, magnificently coifed white-haired woman rested in a wheelchair. She held a cane, clearly a Texan's cane; from it flowed a long suede fringe of deep colors. "Liz Carpenter!" "Yes! that *is* her!"

>Liz,
>once Lady Bird Johnson's
>Staff Director, and
>Press Secretary,

had come to pay her respects; we all honored her space. She smiled my way, and I moved to kneel beside her. She was thinking, she told me, of an LBJ quote: "Education is the only passport out of poverty." Then she added, "and *I* think Barbara *epitomizes* that." She looked once more toward the casket; I silently moved away.

☆♥☆

☆♥☆

I wrote Jacobs, letting him know where his response had led; he replied, recalling the years he and Barbara shared an administrative assistant in their congressional offices. Jacobs added:

"LBJ made a speech to Congress immediately following the Selma tragedy. You will recall that a woman named Viola Liuzzo was murdered during the effort to register people to vote.

"LBJ's prepared speech urging passage of the voting measure was appropriate, but not memorable. His extemporaneous remarks at the end of the speech were both. He said this:

'My first job after college was [as] a teacher in Cotulla, Texas, in a small Mexican-American school. ...They knew even in their youth the pain of prejudice. They never seemed to know why people disliked them. But they knew it was so, because I saw it in their eyes. I often walked home late in the afternoon, after classes were finished, wishing there was more that I could do.

'...I never thought then, in 1928, that I would be standing here in 1965. It never even occurred to me in my fondest dreams that I might have the chance to help the sons and daughters of those students and to help people like them all over this country.

'But now I do have that chance — and I'll let you in on a secret — I mean to use it. And I hope that you will use it with me.'"

Jacobs closed: "It was extraordinarily graceful eloquence for that rough-hewed Texan."

☆♥☆

What do you cherish, from the Sixties?

Healing Ways

☆♥☆

He sat on the small examining stool, white lab coat parting around it; no matter, how many patients to see — up and down the hallway — waiting behind cubicle doors. The question touched him.
      Richard,
        orthopaedic surgeon,
          in Indianapolis, Indiana,
gazed far away, then began speaking slowly, still searching for words. "Faith in shared humanness," he stated. "I still see people *genuinely* concerned for the benefit and welfare of others. I see dedicated physicians here," — he paused — "*many* physicians, surgeons, for whom dealing with *people* is what is important."

This gentle surgeon, who has seen a lifetime of suffering, scores of difficult cases, years of trying to help; this healer still sees the best in our medical profession, and hopes caring doctors will be treating us, tomorrow.

> *1920s —*
> *The Band-Aid was invented by a Johnson & Johnson employee, Eaile Dickson, for his wife.*

☆♥☆

Barbara, massage therapist, specializing in gerontology, in Kerrville, Texas, surprises me. "Medicine!" she emphatically answers. "Tremendous medications that have saved lives...of benefit to mankind." We both laugh. To think the holistic healer treasures the medical advances in our century. The surgeon had said the spirit of man. But then it did make sense; our century is becoming aware of the benefits obtained from both approaches. That these two caretakers of our well-being gave each other's answers shows just how far we've come.

> Merrill, court administrator in Georgetown, TX, treasures our advance in medical cures: "Polio! And cancer. We've come so far!"

Barbara smiles. "It's happening! We keep evolving, on a spiritual level. People *are* opening up, asking a lot of questions. I see a lot of enthusiasm (the God-Spirit within, she explains) in everyone."

What would she like to see, in the next century? "More stewardship of the earth. I'd like for people to have the 'knowingness,' the sort of 'genetic knowledge,' of how to do it. The earth will take care of us; we have to take care of it."

☆♥☆

☆ ♥ ☆

Taking care of family. They say we'll be doing more of it in the future, as the old folks live longer than ever before. And then the adult kids need help, sometimes all at once.

            My friend,
               caretaker for many,
                  lamented on the phone:

"I remember the time I got two emergency messages at once." She was to go out of state and help her ailing mother, when the second call requested aid for her daughter. The young woman needed eye surgery, but who would take care of her, afterward? No matter what my friend would do, she'd be letting one of them down.

"Don't worry, Grandma," her ten-year-old grandson told her. "You take care of *your* mother, and I'll take care of mine."

At that moment, she realized he *could*. Surely he had watched, and learned, the last time his mother had eye surgery. He'd know how to fix an ice pack, when to bring the medicine. He had seen Grandma do it, seen her sit up all night with his Mom, reading Dickens to her to ease the pain.

"That's the point," my friend mused aloud. "In the next century, maybe Medicare will cover less, managed health-care plans already frighten us, and we worry about living longer. I think we have to reach back to our roots, our tradition, and care for our own. I can face the future, if I know someone will sit up with me, reading Charles Dickens."

Sometimes a ten-year-old is absolutely right.

☆♥☆

Jane,
prayer-partner and
writer, living in
Indianapolis, Indiana,
cherishes the family doctor, who faithfully came to the house. She shares one especially grace-filled memory:

"When Grandmother Anna was eighty-six and I was eighteen, she lived with us. My Grandfather James had died three years earlier so it was the natural thing for Anna to make her home with her only remaining daughter.

"Although I had started to college, I commuted daily, and it was fun to come home to Grandmother's gentleness and wonderful sense of humor. We would share a few secrets before dinner as we sat before the fire my Daddy kept burning just for her. I liked hearing about her youth and of how things used to be. We were good companions.

"Anna's only visitor was our family doctor. When Mother called him, Dr. Deever would come, bringing his black bag and tender touch. Attentively he would listen to Grandmother's small complaints, stroke her hand, and sometimes dispense a benign little pill.

Then assuring Mother that all was well, he would accept his small fee and depart. These short visits seemed to make both my grandmother and my mother feel better.

"One day when I bounced through the door and dropped my books I was surprised by what I saw. Anna, who never went out, was bundled up in her ankle-length coat, with her hat pulled down over her ears, sitting on the piano bench in an attitude of waiting. Stunned, I said, 'Are you going out?' Grandmother earnestly responded, 'Your grandpa's coming for me.' That answer sent me scurrying to my mother who assured me that she knew what was going on, and that we shouldn't make too much of it.

"When dinner was on the table, a brief argument occurred because Grandmother did not want to take off her coat. Anna insisted that Jim would 'scotch' at her if she wasn't ready when he got there and reminded my mother of how her Daddy hated to be kept waiting. Mother relented. Anna ate dinner and went off to bed still wrapped in her traveling clothes.

"The next night as this little ritual was being repeated I asked Grandmother *how* Grandpa would come, and was told she 'guessed he'd be in the spring wagon.' This answer brought delightful memories of when I was a child of five. The last mile or two to my grandpa and grandma's home was impassable in our family car, so Daddy would park the car on the highway above the farmstead, honk the horn several times and after a while, Grandpa would come lumbering up in the spring wagon. Excitedly, we would load our boxes and baskets into the wagon and climb in for the bumpy ride down the lane with woods surrounding us and a creek to ford. Thoughts of Grandpa coming this way again gave me a sense of wonder and of peace.

"On the third night before dinner, Mother called Dr. Deever. He arrived just as Grandmother, again in her coat and hat, was tottering off to bed. Taking her arm, he escorted her into her room. As I cleared the table, I could hear them softly talking together.

"Grandmother died that night, passed gently from the arms of the doctor who had cared for her into the arms of my grandpa who had come to fetch her."

☆♥☆

> *Liz, gentle guide in Kerrville, TX, reminds us, "Think of it this way. Although not everyone can choose their coming in, most everyone can take some responsibility for their going out, and therein lies hope for all."*

132

The Music Around Us

☆♥☆

We move into a new century, taking with us the healing words of the surgeon, the advice of a massage therapist, and the challenge of "an enabler of ancient wisdom." Others see healing in our humor, in child's play, our music, and our art.

Harry,
my trombone-playing friend,
in Charlotte, North Carolina,
answered right off: "What I would hug, from this century, is *humor*. My father went through tough times — the Depression, and everything. Mother would say, 'Be funny, Maurice' and he could!" Reflecting a moment, Harry had one more thought on the subject — "Mother was funny, too."

That is obvious; Harry's funny bone was so well nurtured, being around him today is a stitch. Harry had said his hope for the future is that "Our priorities get straightened out, of course, according to *mine*!" Big laugh. Harry always has fun.

☆♥☆

☆♥☆

Michael, corporate editor, in Redmond, Washington, loves computers, trains, music, and children — not always in that order, he adds.

"My children are significantly better for growing up in the 20th Century. We should take pride that we can now indulge our children the freedom to play, to relax, to enjoy leisure.

> "Children will not remember you for the material things you provided, but for the feeling that you cherished them."
> —Robert L. Evans

"In the past one hundred years, children have been freed from the tyranny of long hours at hard labor. What schooling they received was often cut short by the need to assist in supplementing the family's income.

"The sound of children laughing at play is not only a pleasant one, it is the only hope we have." Michael concludes: "And, as they will be rewarded with freedom and love, so shall they bestow these qualities to their children."

☆♥☆

☆♥☆

Judy,
running the garden shop
in Georgetown, Texas,
loves growing things, "plants, and kids!"
　　Judy thinks it is *natural* to children to be outside, to explore!" She loves watching her grandaughter, eating tomatoes off the vine, "pulling, hopefully, weeds!" Judy knows we can't all kneel down in that strawberry patch — "Even if you don't interact, at least you can enjoy being together, outdoors!"

> *"One could not pluck a flower without troubling a star."*
> — *Loren Eiseley*

☆♥☆

What do you do, when you play?

☆♥☆

Little Mandi wants you to reach her *"Take Me Home"* off the top shelf; that's what she calls the dollhouse. Tyler, when he was four, wanted a different slice of watermelon, not the one being offered; "That one has too many *beans* in it!" And this week, Adam asked, "Please, Grandma, can I have that "Moon Over"? I followed his gaze; he wanted the soft-sculpture globe of, as Tyler calls it, "our earth."

I found a pen, put a dot "where we are," another for "Florida"; "Oh boy! Swimmin'! I like it!" Adam crowed.

Adam took the "Moon Over" to bed with him that night. Oh, may the moon over all the grandchildren guard their sleep, and light their way to tomorrow.

☆♥☆

Arisha, a college student, in Kerrville, TX, recalls her own childhood of Barbie dolls, and waiting for the ice cream man to come. She hopes the children of the future "can just be children again, and not have to grow up too fast."

☆♥☆

It was a New Year's Day Tea, with all the little sandwiches and cakes, the silver tea service at the end of the table, the guests milling about. Floating from room to room were the delicate notes plucked from a harp; tinkling spoons and cups, tinkling serenade around them. Mary Catherine, a harpist, in Indianapolis, Indiana, smiled, as she played. Moving closer to her harp, I could feel the floor vibrate with each rippling chord; what was in my ears, entered my soul.

> In 1920, Enrico Caruso gave his last public performance, singing in Halevy's "La Juive" at the Metropolitan Opera, in New York.

Mary Catherine paused, for a short break; we talked. "Oh," she responded, "for the next century, I *hope* we *get back to* music with *harmonious* nuances, not just noise. You know . . . Gershwin, Berlin. I'm a romantic!"

> February 11, 1964 — the Beatles land in New York.

She tilted the harp, raised her arms, and filled the New Year's gathering with harmony. The romantic, playing romance.

☆♥☆

☆♥☆

Marty,
retired, and living in
Venice, Florida,
plays the piano.

These days, Marty plays for retirement homes, nursing homes, her church, her park, "Rotary, club luncheons, etc. — I will, forever."

She writes: "I started when I was six years old and have played ever since. I love it. I started my piano lessons in the first grade. My school had a music teacher who went from school to school and class to class, teaching us all to sing.

"Although I can read music, I learned to play 'by ear' when I was in high school. My brother was in college (we lived in a college town) and he taught me. He played clarinet and had two friends who played 'sax' and guitar. They would come to our house about eleven p.m. and want to have a 'jam session.' We had no music, so we all had to 'play by ear.'"

At eighty-eight, Marty hopes for more for our children than "the violence and sex they are seeing in movies and on TV." She grew up in a "better life." Singing in girl's choruses, taking part in high school musicals such as Gilbert & Sullivan's *Mikado* and *H.M.S. Pinafore*, then later singing in church choirs, with her husband. That is what Marty remembers. And midnight jam sessions with her brother.

Play it, one more time.

☆♥☆

☆♥☆

Winford,
standing just inside an
art gallery window,
in downtown Charlotte,
North Carolina,
is a man of colors. Painting a vibrant portrait of Roger Staubach, he spreads turquoise, crimson, and school-bus-yellow slashes on the canvas. Somehow, the portrait appears; it is magic. I go inside, sit and watch, wait for a moment to speak.

Wiping his brush on a rag, Winford explains: "Every stroke I make on a canvas, everything I do, touch, will *show* 'my color,' what I stand for. I'm an *artist,* to everybody, not a *black* artist."

Winford walks back into the gallery, to find one of his resume flyers for me. I pass other portraits of his, on the gallery walls. I read the names in his folder: "Charles Barkley, Roger Clemens, Muhammad Ali, Michael Jordan, Spike Lee, Derrick McKey, Dale Davis." The folder declares him a world-class artist; it is clear, he is. These are "works singular in spirit," it goes on, "that insist we step in." Color swirls around me.

What does Winford treasure, from this century, and hope for the next? "Nothing we can touch. It's our spirit. Our feelings. Far greater than we know, that can really change lives."

☆♥☆

Use your crayons here — have fun!

☆♥☆

In the spice of life, there is nothing as savory as the sweet music of home. Listen:

Turn the key, the tumblers click just right; you step in. Silence: your special silence. Slight hum of the refrigerator, little metallic tick of the mantle clock. The floor board creaks under the dining room carpet, just as you remember it. Muffled voices from the bedroom above; Kim and Dave are home.

Moving around the apartment, living noises build into your own symphony. Bathtub filling loud and splashy, ding of microwave bell, announcing your mug of strawberry tea is ready. Male late-night talkshow host loud or soft, as you move in and out of your rooms. Whoosh of metal runner, sliding windows open. Now, crickets; and whirr of car tires passing by join in. Creaking of aged wicker hamper, as you replace the lid, over lumpy clothes.

Ah, sweet music of home.

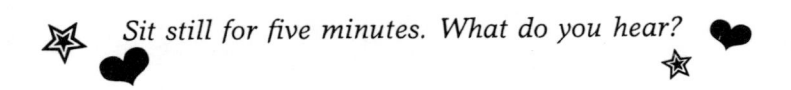

☆♥☆

☆♥ *Sit still for five minutes. What do you hear?* ♥☆

Our Planet

☆♥☆

It was soggy in Knoxville. Dodging fat raindrops, I popped into the store, a haven of candle scent, lilting new-age music, and gifts. Selecting a sea-blue canvas bag with a painted whale curved on an ocean of fabric, I stepped up to the counter to pay.

Jim, owner of the earth-friendly gift shop, in Knoxville, Tennessee, said he originally opened the shop to sell his son's art. I admired the profusion of matted photographs along the brick wall, paid for my bag, and stayed to talk.

"We've made a start in 'the ecology of earth,' he suggested, but we've got a long way to go." Jim leaned on the counter, kept an eye out for customers, and went on: "I remember before strip mining, laying on my belly to drink from Big South Fork River. Fishing. Now, they've cleaned up the process, we've got laws on mining; fishin's good again."

> When a friend complained to Edward Lowe that her cat was tracking ashes from its box all over the house, he got to work, and invented a clay-based absorbent. He named his product "Kitty Litter."

Jim rang up a sale, one soft felt hat to a young woman. He answered a question: "The tee shirts are down this aisle, on the left." Then he had another moment to talk.

"My hope," he said, "is that they will ban all pesticides in twenty-five years." He thought. Then his eyes lit up as he added, "and recognize that tobacco and alcohol are the two worst drugs on earth...*and do away with lobbyists! Period!"*

"That's it. That's my thing to say."

☆♥☆

☆♥☆

Just Add Water

PLANET
is a PLANT
with just one more little "E".
Start with energy
enthusiasm
and expectation.
Planted in earth.
PLANET.

☆♥☆

☆♥☆

Brad,
the avid fly-fisherman,
and insurance adjustor in
Charlotte, North Carolina,
grew up in Syracuse, New York, near the Adirondacks. Brad wants us to treasure silence, and that "a little bit is not bad." He relishes the natural silence comfortable to a fisherman, the time to reflect on how short our life really is. Brad already knows, at twenty-nine, we usually "take ourselves too seriously." He hopes we get back to cherishing our environment "and the rivers we once fished."

> October, 1962, Rachel Carson publishes *Silent Spring* — a book on the harmful effects of pesticides. Her book led to the banning of the use of DDT.

☆♥☆

Patte,
poetry student, and a
college administrator,
in Kerrville, Texas,
hugs beaches and children. "I remember warmly and fondly," she notes, "a clean, uncrowded California beach." Patte knows the sands of time move swiftly: "Hug your children just one more time; before you know it, you are hugging your grandchildren." Patte hopes there will be clean beaches, for those little ones to run on.

Our Faith

☆ ♥ ☆

"In God we Trust" is still on the back of every U.S. one dollar bill; we seldom look at it. In today's hectic world, some say we are losing touch with our spiritual base. How are the people of the next century going to deal with all the economic, political, or environmental troubles we see around us?
     United Methodist Bishop,
     Reuben P. Job,
     living near Nashville, Tennessee,
believes there *is* an "assurance of a presence" that transforms even our weakness "into gifts of service." Bishop Job challenges us to "a much more radical discipleship," asks us to stop wondering "What does it cost?" or "What is in it for us?" and begin to ask "What does God want us to do?"

  I met Bishop Job last fall, at a retreat center where he was the invited speaker. "My sense is," he spoke, "we are still trying to do what we've always done." This gentle, wise leader continued through the day; my notebook filled.

  Bishop Job neared the end of his presentation;

he looked up more often, for emphasis: "*How* are we being called to respond to the broken world?" He looked around the room. "Be a healing presence; stand with the wounded, and *offer*. Be a sacrificial presence — not in the sense of courting martyrdom, but more as a response, a service. Be a reconciling presence that begins to repair, to make ties and form bonds.

"*How* do we live out discipleship in a broken world?" he asks. "See God, in the faces around you. Make this a way of *life*, each day."

At the end of the day, Bishop Job said he would think about the questions for this book, and respond. His letter arrived:

> *Barb, Bill, and Leonard, at Saranac Lake, New York, hope "we return to some kind of faith, because that has sustained us for centuries."*

"I suppose one of the most important things for us to remember from this century is that the darkness has not overcome the light. In spite of two world wars, famine, natural destruction, and disease, the light, goodness and truth of God continue.

"My hope for the coming century is that there will be a great religious awakening that sweeps the globe turning men, women and children toward God in new and wonderful ways. This I believe would result in a new awareness of our interdependence as human family."

☆❤☆

☆♥☆

Shirley,
the friend of my sister,
and now, a metaphysical learner
in Potomac, Maryland,
echoes Bishop Job's hope. Oh, we use different language across our land, but there is a shared ground swell of hope. Shirley writes:

"I hope the recognition of spiritual energy begun in the early decades of recorded history and rediscovered in the 20th Century will gain worldwide acceptance and use as a healing power. Spirituality based on common metaphysical principles will unite the peoples of the earth."

☆♥☆

> *"Listen for the sound of the genuine within yourself and others. Meditate and learn to be alone without being lonely."*
> *— Marian Knight Edelman*

☆♥☆

Move on down to Texas; meet
    guitar-playing song writer
    Sherry,
    of Kerrville.
Sherry treasures the "ebb and flow, as we join universal cycles of create/destroy/create/destroy to higher and higher levels." A psychologist, by trade, Sherry incorporates spirit in her music, and her healing art. "Increasing validity to the inner journey" is her hope for us ahead.

☆♥☆

> *Tony Kushner, in a sermon at the Cathedral of St. John the Divine, in New York asks: "Must grace fall so unevenly on the earth? . . . We perish for the lack of lively rain. There's a drought for want of grace everywhere."*

☆♥☆

My minister included some words in one of his sermons that caught my attention: "There *is* a God-shaped reservoir of unfathomable depth,...an abundance...a sufficiency."

☆♥☆

This abundance is what excites
    Jay,
    professor of religion,
    and a writer,
    in Indianapolis, Indiana.

She believes, and teaches that "We should remember, cherish, and hug our Scriptures. They are our guide to living faithfully, every day as we move toward the end of this century. They enable us to sense God in our world." Jay wrote to me, sharing her personal hope:

"I hope, in my lifetime, that archaeologists find the lost Book of Elijah. Some scholars think that such a book existed and that the Elijah stories we have in 1 and 2 Kings are from this book. From these stories Elijah appears as a man of great mental,

> *In 1968, the Apollo 8 astronauts, orbiting the moon, read passages from the Old Testament Book of Genesis, during a Christmas Eve television broadcast.*

physical, and spiritual strength and determination. He is totally given over to God, so much so that, when it was time for him to die, God swept him away from earth in a chariot of fire.

"As 1 Kings 17 opens there is Elijah bigger than life! He appears abruptly and goes right to work. 'Wait a minute,' I want to shout. 'What about his background? What led to his relationship with God? How was he called to be a prophet?' Then, after we read of his encounters with Ahab, Jezebel, and the prophets of Baal, I really want more information. 'What events and experiences helped make him the bold and obedient man he was?'

"Elijah is a mystery man, to say the least. I admire him. I am in awe of him. I think I would like him if he were around today (although his intensity might get to me). Above all, I want more bits of information to complete my picture of him. Until that happens, he will remain an exemplar of the faith for me."

☆♥☆

☆♥☆

Sue,
my other beloved
college roommate,
long a Montessori teacher,
now lives in Bensalem,
Pennsylvania.

Sue treasures "Inspirational books! That is," she writes, in response to my questions, "*Chicken Soup for the Soul, The Road Less Traveled,* etc. — and others too numerous to mention!" Sue savors the fact that these books "remain on the best seller lists while the more secular/sensationalistic fiction and non-fiction 'garbage' have their brief moments in the limelight and then thankfully die out.

> *"I don't pray. Kneeling bags my nylons."*
> — 1951 movie *The Big Carnival,* starring Jan Sterling

"Our overstressed society," Sue continues, "refuses to give up but continues seeking solutions to painful problems through caring volunteer workers, intensive medical research, groups dedicated to environmental concerns, etc. To many people, our society appears impersonal and full of selfish, even evil and inhumane citizens, but seeking out the good in society will inevitably turn up more 'good apples' than rotten ones."

☆♥☆

☆♥☆

Where do we find food for spirit? Everywhere. Just listen to

>Nancy,
>sales representative,
>mother, and dear friend,
>living in Charlotte,
>North Carolina.

"Waterfalls." And, she adds, giggling, "Watermelon!"

Her mood becomes serious, as she explains. "I collect watermelons now; I love them. Salt and pepper shakers, refrigerator magnets, notepaper...anything."

Seems years ago, Nancy had been working at the local "Methodist Home." It had been an exhausting day; all day, Nancy held on to the thought that "this afternoon, when I get done, I can go to the watermelon fest." Late in the day, Nancy didn't notice there was one more family, one more intake process, to be handled.

"What are you going to do now?" she was asked.

"I'm going *outside*! To the fest!" And she did, believing her work was done.

Gracious co-workers covered that case and never

got to the fest themselves. Later, Nancy knew how blessed she was. Today, she keeps watermelon symbols, as reminders.

The waterfalls? Nancy offers us that image: "Take your cares, and throw them in!" she says. "Throw them far, where you can't ever get them back." It always works, for her.

☆♥☆

Silence . . . waterfalls . . . where is your place to encounter Spirit?

Our Tomorrow

☆♥☆

"Tomorrow's hopes begin by remembering yesterday."
— artist Paul Fierlinger,
in his memoirs.

☆♥☆

There is one treasure to add, one more hope for tomorrow:
Sue,
mother of my new
daughter-in-law,
is a singer, and a bicyclist,
in Auburn, Indiana.
With profound simplicity, Sue suggests "Each of us should *remember* to *remember*. Often life is so hectic, we don't have the time or attitude to reflect. So take time to recall with thankfulness and *remember*."

☆♥☆

Have you added to the book, writing in your thoughts? Are you now talking about hugs and hopes for the century, with your family? Then here's my invitation: keep it growing! Call your cousin, have tea with your neighbor. Everyone has something to add.

Let's celebrate the good we bring to a new century, together.

☆♥☆

"We preserve what we find useful or beautiful or true . . . we make of what we have found the hope of our immortality."
— Lewis H. Lapham

Sara Sanderson is an Indianapolis essayist, poet, lecturer, and book reviewer. She has written commissioned lyrics for internationally performed music, most of which is published here in the States. For the *Hugs & Hopes* collection, she traveled over two thousand miles and interviewed people ages seven to ninety-three.